Martin James Childs - 2004

Martin James Childs - 2004

The Platinum Years

designed by Albert Squillace

A Ridge Press Book

THE PLATINUM YEARS

by Bob Willoughby / Text by Richard Schickel

Studio Vista

Studio Vista
Cassell & Collier Macmillan Publishers Ltd.,
35 Red Lion Square, London WC1R 4SG

ISBN 0 289 70632 7

Printed by Mondadori Editore, Verona.

Contents

The Platinum Years were a very special time. In Hollywood, my home town, they were an era of lush, spectacular films, but also an era of foundation-shaking changes in the motion-picture industry: the collapse of the studio system and its constellations of stars, the emergence of the independently-produced film, and the rise of television with its bag of mixed blessings. Eventually, the platinum lost its dazzle, and the kind of movies and production style it implied simply disappeared, swept under by the contemporary trend to low-budget, no-star, auteur pictures.

All these factors had a bearing on my participation in the Platinum Years—these plus the gradual demise of the large-circulation national magazines.

In the early fifties, as I was starting, about the biggest publicity push the studios could give a film was to have it previewed in **Life, Look, Collier's, This Week, Redbook, McCall's,** or **Harper's Bazaar,** in color if possible, and the more pages the better. The stories were fun to do, they were popular, and they paid well. Every top-drawer photographer—staff or free-lance—took a crack at them at one time or another.

I got into this competitive scramble because Charles Bloch, then West Coast editor of Globe Photos, saw an exhibition of my work at a little La Cienega cinematheque and was enthusiastic enough to show samples to Alexei Brodovich, the talented art director of **Harper's Bazaar.** Alexei gave me my first film assignments: Claire Bloom, then appearing in

Chaplin's **Limelight,** Danny Kaye's **Hans Christian Andersen,** Richard Burton in **The Desert Rats.**

Eventually, as TV cut into the advertising dollars allocated to print, the magazines began to pare their West Coast photo bureaus. And free lances like me–"specials," we were called–were hired by the studios to maneuver for the magazine publicity space they were finding it harder and harder to get.

Working on a set, of course, is quite different from working in your own studio. You have total control in your studio, none at all on the set. You are completely at the mercy of the production process, the director's authority, the stars' temperaments. On small sets–for instance, the apartment rooms used in **Petulia** and **Rosemary's Baby**–there is literally nowhere for a photographer to squeeze in with the technical crew and find the viewpoints he might wish. On large sets–**The Great Race, Catch-22, They Shoot Horses**–there is so much going on, and the scale is so vast, that it's difficult to know where or when to set up. Some directors are cooperative; they welcome the still photographer's presence. Some feel he is an intrusion on an already complicated and costly process, a distraction to the actors from whom he is trying to elicit a mood and a performance.

Worst of all is the eternal waiting. Movie making must be one of the slowest procedures ever devised by man. Hours go by and there's not a thing you can do to speed things up.

To overcome some of the physical problems on the set, I had to design or develop a considerable amount of special gear. In conjunction with Irving Jacobsen, I built the first effective sound blimp for a 35mm still camera. I further designed a great group of clamps and brackets which enabled me to attach my camera to the movie camera itself, to zero in on situations from which I was necessarily distant, and to compensate for the impossibility of being three places at once. I helped get the bugs out of the first radio-controlled camera used on a film. I've had my cameras and lenses modified to suit my particular needs, and I've really bent over backwards to resolve the various problems that each new film seemed to offer.

Mostly, however, the Platinum Years were marvelous ones for me. And in putting this book together–in looking once again at the twenty years of photography it represents–I was warmed by recollections of all the people who shared these experiences with me: editors, reporters, and fellow photographers from the magazines; publicity men, directors, actors, and crews from the movie world; Lee Gross, my former agent, who for fourteen years fought for and won more space for the studios in national publications than anyone before or after; and Steve Hansen and his sidekick, the late Eddie Laguna, who processed and printed every picture in this book with care, patience, and understanding.

–B.W.
Coolmaine Castle
County Cork, Ireland

The Platinum Years by Richard Schickel

Platinum implies excess. In any sensible society, gold–blessed with its traditional status–should be sufficient as a measure of value, and the desire to find some metal (and some metaphor) symbolizing still greater marvels of creative effort or rarity is bound to strike persons of conservative taste as pointless. Perhaps even as a sign of moral decline.

So there is a certain intentional irony in our title. Yet it is also in my opinion a precisely accurate description of the era of American film history impressionistically recorded by Bob Willoughby's camera and herewith offered in book form. The reasons for this opinion are several and require an explanation.

We all know that starting around 1950 the American film industry entered upon hard times economically, that it has never succeeded entirely in freeing itself from the constraints under which it was therefore forced to operate, and probably never will. Certainly no one any longer supposes anything like a restoration of the old days of power and profitability is about to take place. It would be dismal to repeat at length the standard analysis of what brought Hollywood to its once and future pretty pass. Suffice it to say that an antitrust suit forced the studios to divest themselves of their profitable and economically stabilizing theater chains, and that the arrival of television, providing free the routine entertainment formerly supplied by program pictures, disrupted the national habit of going to the movies regularly and without paying any particular attention to what was offered there. One should also note that, even without the presence of television, affluence would probably have diminished the audience for films, for in the fifties we began spending more time with more expensive leisure pursuits–on our boats, at our country clubs, in our weekend homes.

The results of all this were predictable. The number of admissions to movie houses sold each week dropped between 1950 and the late sixties by something like two-thirds–from around seventy-five million a week to something under twenty-five million. The number of movies produced by the major studios was, not surprisingly, cut in half, though there was a partially offsetting rise in the number of films imported, a reflection of the changing interests of the remaining audience for movies. The old mass audience had essentially disappeared, though it could be lured forth for special attractions of the sort not commonly available on TV–large-scale spectacles, for example, or pictures which promised "adult" treatment either of sexual matters or of ideas. Or, as we shall see in the following pages, certain entertainments that might provide the centerpiece for a family outing.

The regular moviegoers of the fifties and sixties tended to be younger, better educated, with larger cultural aspirations than had formerly been the case. By and large, they had persuaded themselves that film was, or should be, an art form. They were, many of them, less interested in stars than in directors (who, they had come to understand, were central figures in the creative process of making a film) and they appreciated novelty–or at least the show of it–in a way that was quite different from that of the old audience. The old audience, whether it consciously knew it or not, was more interested in renewing itself by staying in touch with certain film forms and film figures which had, through repeated exposure, taken on something like mythic proportions. It was, in fact, annoyed by excesses of invention.

This is not to say, of course, that American movie makers entirely abandoned their traditional forms and it is not to imply that they did not invent, especially in the sixties, new genres—or new variations of the older genres—which exerted a quasi-mythic fascination on some segments of the audience. Stories about sensitive young men, pushed into rebellion against "the system" were, for example, often enough commercially successful to make them seem for a while safe gambles to producers. Lately, stories about the unhappy lot of policemen have been well received at the box office and, though they have links to an earlier breed of "policier," they differ significantly from them in their concern for internal corruption and in their frequent emphasis on a redefined criminal element—drug pushers, political radicals, psychopaths, very different from the gangster as he was defined in the films of the thirties. Similarly, the western genre has been updated. Movies in this category now tend to be about the closing of the frontier rather than about the opening of it, as was formerly the case.

The important thing about all this activity, the most obvious thread running through the history of the American cinema over the last couple of decades, is the fact that all movies cost more than in the past, and that this was not merely, or mainly, a function of the generally inflationary economy in which they were made. Very simply, moviegoing ceased to be a habit which could be fed by mostly interchangeable products, and individual movies therefore had to give the impression of being an event. It is true, of course, that from **Marty** (1955) onward, many predicted that small, inexpensive films, the very cheapness of which served as an earnest of their sober intentions, would—and probably should—become the dominant element in the studios' production schedules and, indeed, quite a few of them did prosper in the marketplace. The trouble was that cheapness confined the

film maker to realism of a gritty and unromantic sort and no one wanted that as a regular diet. Romance, adventure, above all, nostalgia, are expensive to create on screen, and despite the variations worked on the traditional plots and characters during this period, even the new audience wanted these qualities in their films, no matter what else they might pretend.

Finally, with fewer pictures being made, each separate film was required to contribute more to paying such fixed (and, after a certain point, apparently irreducible) costs as overhead. It made sense, therefore, to spend more on each individual film in an attempt (often useless) to insure its acceptance. In short, each film represented a much bigger gamble than had ever been the case before. A studio could—and often did—lose millions on a picture, and without exception all were at various points in the fifties and sixties forced to the wall—sometimes, as in the case of Metro-Goldwyn-Mayer with **Ben Hur** and **Mutiny on the Bounty** and Fox with **Cleopatra,** as the result of cost overruns on one or two films.

On the other hand, if the potentials for loss were higher than ever, so were potential winnings. On the list of all-time box-office champions published annually by "Variety," only one film made prior to 1950 (**Gone With the Wind**) is in the top ten. Indeed, one has to go all the way to fifty-sixth place (where **Snow White** has carved its niche) to find another pre-fifties production. By and large, these big winners grossed much larger amounts—$20 or $25 million and more, as opposed to $3 or $4 million for the hits of the thirties and forties. The movies have always been a game for high rollers, but never had the game provided the thrills and spills of the past two decades.

And that, of course, is where

platinum, or at least platinum-plating, comes in. The very small handful of stars who could actually bring people into the theater on the basis of their names, no matter what the title underneath, commanded huge salaries (up to $1 million) against equally heavy percentages of the picture's gross. With this kind of "above the line" investment it seemed sensible to make their vehicles match their salaries in expense. Everything from the costumes to the locations went up in price, and any number of the films that returned astronomical grosses–say, $15 million– and now rest comfortably on the upper levels of that "Variety" chart actually lost money for their producers. Many others returned smaller profits than pictures of the thirties and forties which grossed–at smaller admission prices–only a few million dollars.

Aside from this remarkable and unprecedented emphasis on cost, are there any other tendencies one can isolate among the American movies of the last twenty or twenty-five years, tendencies that tell us something about ourselves rather than about the economic conditions of the motion-picture industry?

Naturally, the economic situation within the industry distorted everything, making it difficult to clearly read the images of ourselves held up by the film mirror. Nevertheless, I think we do find some more or less constant preoccupations in the films of our period. Many of these will be taken up in greater detail in the comments on specific movies which follow. But here we might note that overall there was a stylistic change in movie making so massive that critics like Andrew Sarris have taken to calling the style of previous periods "classical," discreetly not giving a name to the mess that has followed. Basically, except in movies that aim to recapture, if only for a night, the old mass

audience, directors have taken to seeing the world in subjective rather than objective terms. In various, largely technical ways, they impose upon us in their choice of imagery, in their cutting rhythms, almost subliminally, their highly personal views of the world. They make their statements about the human condition, often as not, by the way they see, rather than through their choice of what they see. The implication of this change in style is that the objectivity of the classical style is no longer usefully revelatory. Objectivity was possible because there was a common unspoken agreement among directors and audience as to what the basic shape and condition of the world and its citizens were. We needed very little help or guidance to understand the director's assumptions about his characters or the moral landscape they inhabited. Essentially we shared an optimistic view of humankind and a strong sense of what constituted good and evil in people. Things were clear cut. Now these basic assumptions have been called into general question. Each individual has had to define the world for himself, and certainly any movie director who claims to be an artist has had to do so. Indeed, in so doing the director is able, belatedly, to join the entire modernist tradition–distinctly not a realistic tradition–enunciated early in the century in the other arts, but late in gaining influence in a film world which clung to the old-fashioned narrative traditions of the Victorian theater and novel.

The upshot of this has been a film style fragmentary in its imagery, very often lacking in a powerful storytelling drive, as well as in boldly, broadly fashioned characters. More and more, especially in the sixties, directors, by the showiness of their styles, the suggestion of anguished searching in their methods, called attention to themselves and to the primacy of their role as creators. And as—of all things—thinkers, philosophers. That much of what they offered was impossibly sophomoric, or giddily misanthropic, or simply stupid by any standard more educated than that of the deep-dish show-biz set did not seem to matter. After all, much of their audience was youthful. Or if it was not that, then it was half-educated, bringing to the moviegoing experience the half-remembered catchwords of freshman survey courses in existentialism—"alienation," "anomie," that sort of thing. Real depth was not a requisite with this crowd; only its appearance was.

Side by side, indeed, often mixed in thoroughly with this view there was, especially as the sixties wore on, a profound nostalgia for older, simpler times. Hence the popularity of period pieces, even of films like the three run up by Peter Bogdanovich in which he carefully resurrected something like the old-movie style, seeming to pay homage to the classical masters of our cinema, as his critical friends would have it, simply ripping them off as his enemies believed. No matter, almost any movie that took us back to times most of the audience wasn't able to actually remember, but which had come to look very attractive to them as they lived through the profoundly disturbing sixties, was likely to prove profitable. Even if the olden times were evoked mockingly, as camp, those films that did so were likely to draw crowds.

It was perfectly true that, while the majority of films were financed through the studios, most were "independent productions," although this independence proved to be less liberating aesthetically and spiritually than those who had dreamed of it, back in the days of factory-like studio productions, imagined it would be. The marketplace, though shrunken, was still a marketplace and it was conducted much as it had always been. Success continued to breed imitation. We were no less afflicted by genre cycles than we ever had been. Consciously or unconsciously, styles which proved popular were aped. And dominant directors and actors, whether they were actually any good or not, continued to get the most work, to dominate—often boringly—our screens.

But there were worse defects in the new system. Our range of choice was greatly curtailed. Fewer films (and fewer theaters) meant that all movies, good and bad, tended to hang about longer. The quick, deft, light entertainments of former years—the kind of unpretentious little pictures that one often discovered without help from critics and the rest of the publicity machinery—simply were no more. Indeed, one often saw multimillion-dollar productions which seemed to contain within themselves the germs of just such pleasant little experiences, but which clanked laboriously, stupidly about under the weight of their...well, their platinum-plating. They were overproduced and underthought. Again, many movies of more modest scope were distorted by sensation-seeking, bursts of meaningless violence, for example, or sexual encounters where the problem was not in itself the nudity that seemed to weigh so heavily on the puritanical mind in these years, but the misogyny and the general kinkiness the camera lingered over so lovingly. In sum, one nowadays often feels pummelled as one emerges from the theater, battered by the conspicuous consumption of the producers or by their frantic search for new sensations which they hope will enable them to gain a toehold in the choosy new market for movies. Or both.

One does not lust mindlessly for the dear, dead days. There was so much that was banal and inept on our screens in the thirties and forties. And, indeed, in every year of the modern film era there has been at least a handful of films that are as fine as the finest of previous eras. Many of them, moreover, are excellent in entirely new ways, for there can be no doubt that the freedom to tackle previously forbidden subject matter with new stylistic tools has opened the screen to new realms of experience. One might, indeed, summarize by saying that the percentage of genuinely good films and genuinely bad ones has remained relatively constant through the years, that where we seem now to have lost out is in the middle range. You used to be able to find, on a given lonely or boring evening, something you could comfortably, in a holiday spirit, merely enjoy; something which might surprise or delight or instruct in an unpretentious way, something which might actually live on, as so many of the program features of the thirties and forties have, to enliven TV's late shows in a manner that the more heralded films of their times do not. It is in this range, I think, that the genius of American film making lay. Certainly it was from this range (a range incidentally which television does not approximate in quality or intelligence) that the actors and directors we most cherish emerged in the past. And, in fact, it was the range within which the great audience, now lost, learned a fairly sophisticated appreciation of the possibilities of movies.

The book you are now holding does not pretend to be a complete and balanced survey of the approximately two decades it covers. Bob Willoughby is an expert and highly valued still photographer, and he covered many of the era's most popular and most distinguished productions. But no one man can be expected to have covered everything of significance that Hollywood turned out. Still, his work does support most of the generalizations one feels most com-

pelled to make about the movies of this time span. More important, one gains from his photographs a sense of the backstage excitement, that peculiar blend of hope, energy, and concern that attends the making of any movie. The decision to make a movie may be a cynical or a wrong-headed one. The final result may disappoint no one so much as the people who created the film. But while the work proceeds, there is no more fascinating—or all-consuming—endeavor available to men and women of temperament and talent. If some of the evaluations of their work is bleak, as in all honesty they must be, Bob Willoughby's pictures offset those judgments, capture that spirit that has made some of us—even those who are mere critical hangers-on—forever movie crazy, no matter how impatient or irritable a given film may make us.

From Here to Eternity
1953

From Here to Eternity was a movie that filled a lot of people with hope. When it was released in 1953 it seemed it might represent the culmination of the drive—mostly fueled by the cultural aspirations of middle-brow critics and the middle-class audience—for a new, higher seriousness in the movies. In the years since World War II other films had prepared the way for it: **Treasure of the Sierra Madre, All the King's Men, Sunset Boulevard, All About Eve, A Place in the Sun, The Red Badge of Courage,** and, from the man who directed **Eternity,** Fred Zinnemann, **The Men** and **High Noon.** Many of these films were adaptations of literary classics which another generation of

Adding the Zinnemann touch.

movie makers would have hesitated to mix with. All, no matter what their source, were praised as "literate" and welcomed for their ambitions. Quite a few were commercial successes and, therefore, the recipients of many Academy Award nominations and no small number of Oscars (**Eternity** received eight of them).

The result of all this activity was much talk about a new "maturity" in the American film, a maturity which many of its champions hoped would, given a little time for the maturity to mature, result in movies that would match the exemplary sobriety of the Italian Neo-realists, much in fashion among a public which liked to think of itself as discriminating. The other films in this new category seemed to me then, and seem to me even more so in retrospect, a very mixed blessing. They carried, very often and not very gracefully, a heavy load of intellectual freight and tended to talk too much and be both too earnest and too self-conscious

about their self-appointed duty to bring culture and enlightenment to the masses.

From Here to Eternity escaped these pitfalls. To begin with, it was based on a book which, though more interesting and more deeply felt than the average best seller, was in no danger of being misunderstood as a truly great work. It merely had an honest story to tell about a group of people—professional soldiers in peacetime—for whom most of us had not spared a thought, allowing us to penetrate a closed, exotic world. From James Jones' sprawling, award-winning best seller, Daniel Taradash fashioned an expert adaptation for the screen, faithful to the spirit of the novel but shaped with far greater care than the original work, giving it the main thing it lacked, graceful proportions. In his turn, Zinnemann, who has a marvelous eye for composition, created shot after shot, sequence after sequence, that was visually right without being showy or calling particular attention to the director's skill. One thinks of the opening sequence, which not only familiarizes us quickly with the locale (the prison-like Schofield Barracks in Hawaii), but efficiently establishes the film's theme as well. For we catch our first glimpse of its hero, that determined individualist, Robert E. Lee Prewitt (Montgomery Clift) striding alone against a huge flow of humanity—hundreds and hundreds of drilling soldiers. It is his battle against this regimented tide that will form the substance of the film and the source of its undying appeal.

This subject, of course, was particularly potent in the early fifties, when McCarthyism was a particularly noxious force in American society, but the drama of the man who dares to stand out against the crowd has long been a recurring one in every genre of American films. Thus, despite the unique setting and the highly original characters on view, **Eternity** also served to link the new seriousness of the American film to a good, older tradition in American movie making. In short, it was at once fresh and comforting in the sense of continuity with our movie past which it imparted.

Indeed, the film's most famous performance was marked by this Janus-like quality. At the time everyone knew that Frank Sinatra, his career as a crooner in disarray, had campaigned desperately for his first serious dramatic role, that of the tough, tragic Maggio, who dies rather than allow the brutality of the stockade to break his spirit. It was understood that Sinatra, the one-time teen-age rage, had staked everything on his success in this part and, of course, he surprised many people with his appealing performance. Some of the vulnerable charm that had been more apparent to his adolescent wartime fans than to their parents came across to adults for the first time in this film. So did the strength and intelligence which was to propel him from near has-been status to that central position in the show-biz hierarchy which he would occupy for the next two decades—a gifted, shrewd, difficult, loved, feared, powerful personality whose comings and goings, both socially and politically, would preoccupy the populace more than any of the starring roles he would essay in film, on television, and in the clubs and concert halls in the fifties and sixties.

It is fair to say, in fact, that none of the performers in **From Here to Eternity** ever again achieved the artistic success that came to them in this film. Burt Lancaster and Deborah Kerr, as the master sergeant and the officer's lady whose love forced them across caste lines, never found anything more suitable than these roles, though they were, of course, major stars of the period. Donna Reed, who, like Sinatra, won a supporting performer Oscar as the romantic hooker, reverted to her former too-nice type as the star of her own television show. Ernest Borgnine, wonderfully evil as Sinatra's nemesis, Fatso Judson, changed his image with **Marty** and has never been so incisive again. Clift's handsome visage would be marred in an auto accident and he never found anything as powerful or as fine as Prewitt (or as Matthew Garth in the earlier **Red River**).

As for Fred Zinnemann, always a slow and careful worker, he would make a succession of slow and careful—if visually attractive—films during the next twenty years, but he never found anything as dramatically strong or as emotionally astringent as **From Here to Eternity.** In the new age of independent production, the stabilizing role of the studios, with their long-term contractual interest in finding suitable vehicles for their talent, was diminished. Like all truly fine, truly memorable films of the period, therefore, **Eternity** was a magnificent accident —essentially unduplicable.

The Caine Mutiny

1953

Herman Wouk's **The Caine Mutiny** was one of the great media phenomena of the fifties: a best-selling novel, a hit play, and finally (in 1953) a successful movie produced by earnest, heavy-handed, liberaloid Stanley Kramer, one of the leaders of the movement toward independent production and a great proponent of the new seriousness in movies.

It is not hard to understand why **The Caine Mutiny** was a story the middle brows reacted to as children do to a favorite fairy tale, demanding to have it told over and over again. It was basically a good, strong narrative, tracing the descent of Captain Queeg–who became an archetypal representative of this kind of craziness– into paranoia, a condition that finally necessitated, or so it seemed to a liberal intellectual serving under him (well played in the film by Fred MacMurray), his involuntary surrender of command of his minesweeper, the U.S.S. Caine. It was this man, Lt. Keefer, who convinced the rest of the junior officers in the wardroom to relieve Queeg during the height of a typhoon, an action which led to the trial–and eventual acquittal–of the executive officer on charges of mutiny.

The strength of Wouk's narrative would have meant little, however, had it not led his characters and his audience to a confrontation with A Great Moral Issue. As Dwight MacDonald, among others, has observed, such confrontations are absolutely essential to success with the middle-brow audience, whose aesthetic has not advanced much beyond realism, but which feels somehow cheated if the work at hand does not lead to consideration of some big question or problem. With the supposedly thoughtless mass audience lost to television, this smaller but more intense crowd became, in the fifties and sixties, absolutely essential to the commercial success of a film–or, indeed, to any artistic product in any medium which aspired to large profitability.

The Issue which concerned Wouk was, considering the historical moment, a pip. What could have been more appropriate to the early fifties than a discussion of the individual's relationship to authority? What could have been more comforting than his conclusion that mutinies (and revolts), however justifiable–and the case against Queeg was impressive–were

not to be countenanced? For this was, after all, the decade of the silent generation and the lonely crowd and the organization man, a time when the cultural critics were endlessly concerned with an obvious trend toward conformity of all sorts and at every level of society. On the college campuses the political fervency of the immediate past had been stilled. In the adult world masses of people were quietly fitting themselves into corporate niches, trading off individuality for what seemed to be guaranteed, lifelong prosperity. Politically, the passive Eisenhower had replaced peppery Harry Truman, and everyone seemed glad enough simply to let the problems pile up for eight years. Then, of course, there was McCarthyism, terrifying people into silence on all sorts of political and, indeed, moral issues.

In this atmosphere of quietude Wouk's message–that obedience to author-

Van Johnson takes a typhoon break

ity, however crackbrained, was preferable to deposing that authority—was a comforting one for a lot of people, particularly since his long work gave the impression that he had carefully considered the matter, given both sides in the argument a fair shake. Whether, in fact, he did so is open to serious question. The mutineer Maryk is defended in his court-martial by one Barney Greenwald, who gets him off by forcing Queeg to break down emotionally on the witness stand. Later, however, Greenwald excoriates his client and his cohorts. Whatever Queeg's inadequacies, he says, the man had devoted his life to manning democracy's ramparts during the period between the wars, while his tormentors were devoting themselves to their own selfish interests. Without men like Queeg, Greenwald tells them, they would not have been free to so indulge themselves, and he, Greenwald, a Jew, might have seen his grandmother turned into "a bar of soap" (as Wouk inelegantly puts it) had not men like Queeg been willing to form part of a deterrent shield, causing Hitler and his allies to hesitate to attack.

The argument seems preposterous. One can, after all, appreciate the contributions to our safety by career military men without arguing that all of them—no matter how loony—are entitled to exemption from responsibility for their behavior as individuals. Similarly, one can respect authority and the traditions it may represent without arguing, as Wouk seemed to, that we owe it blind and total obedience. One might even argue that respect for it is enhanced by showing that, when its errors are grievous, machinery exists within the system to responsibly challenge it. (There is, after all, a Navy regulation that permits junior officers to relieve a superior of command when he shows himself no longer fit to exercise it, which is precisely the regulation under which the "mutineers" acted.) There is also, in retrospect, something unpleasant about using a Jew to advance the argument for obedience. Within a decade the Eichmann case would come to public attention and his defense would be simply that he had obeyed orders in overseeing the "processing" of hundreds of thousands of Jews to and through Hitler's death camps. Would Wouk, himself a Jew, have extended his argument for Queeg to include Eichmann? Finally, what is one to make of Wouk's portrait of the intellectual, Keefer, as a slippery, cowardly troublemaker? One does not, of course, argue that intellectuals are any more righteous than other citizens, but in a period in which the breed was under attack from yahoos like McCarthy, there was something unseemly, if not socially irresponsible, about Wouk's representation of it—and other "types" as well—in his fiction.

These questions are, perhaps, feckless. **The Caine Mutiny** was very much a product of its historical moment. Its afterlife has been terribly short, and one feels fairly confident in suggesting that it will remain no more than an historical footnote to one of the drearier chapters in the nation's modern history. Still, one cannot leave the footnote without adding a footnote to it. The film was directed by Edward Dmytryk. He had been one of the original Hollywood Ten, and he had been jailed for refusing to answer the questions posed him by the House Un-American Activities Committee when it was pursuing its fantasy that Hollywood had been a hotbed of subversives before and during World War II. Having done his time like a good fellow, however, Dmytryk did a turnabout, naming the people who allegedly had been members of the Communist Party back in the bad old days. Having submitted to this degrading process, he was free to work in pictures again, and there is a rather heavy irony in the fact that his first major production was this argument in favor of truckling to authority. One would like to say that, given his circumstances, he brought a certain intensity of feeling to his work. Alas, it was not so. There were good performances in addition to MacMurray's–notably Bogart as Queeg and Van Johnson as the likeable Maryk–but the film was as routine as the many "B" pictures Dmytryk had done before, as plodding as the many earnest but undistinguished large-scale productions he was to handle.

A Star Is Born

1954

A Star Is Born is the quintessential show-biz legend. It intertwines the stories of two archetypal figures of the endlessly fascinating celebrity drama as it was invented and practiced in America in our century: Judy Garland as the star on the rise, James Mason as the star destroying himself precisely because he cannot handle the fame to which she, more or less innocently, aspires.

Directed by George Cukor with his customary grace and elegance, this 1954 film is, of course, a remake of William A. Wellman's 1937 production of the same name and that, in its turn, owed something to a 1932 picture Cukor had also directed, **What Price Hollywood?**–which suggests how, through the years, the themes explored here have preoccupied show people. (Indeed, there is an even more curious coincidence to relate. Around the time Wellman and writer Robert Carson were working on the original story for the first **A Star Is Born,** Cukor visited his old friend John Barrymore in a depressing "rest home," where the actor was attempting to gain control of his alcoholism. Cukor offered him a small part in one of his pictures but was turned down. He told producer David O. Selznick about this rather unsettling experience and Selznick in turn told Wellman, who saw to it that a similar scene was worked into his film. He even used some of the dialogue as it had been reported to him. Then, in 1954, when he did the remake, Cukor found himself directing a new version of the scene in which he had been an original participant.)

On the whole, his picture is more interesting than Wellman's even though–except for the musical numbers–it follows the original very closely. The reason for this lies partly in the fact that the songs are very excitingly done and make the work more flashily show-biz than its predecessor. Mostly, however, it is because Cukor was more fortunate than Wellman in his casting. In the 1937 film Fredric March, generally an exciting screen presence, played the declining Norman Maine very conservatively–almost as if he were afraid a full-out portrait of a self-destructive actor would hurt his image. Janet Gaynor, as Esther Blodgett/Vicki Lester, was mostly merely soppy. In contrast, James Mason, an actor of superb daring, who has always seemed to relish the opportunity to paint in broad, bold slashes, gave a performance larger than life–a well-observed near-caricature of an actor trying to turn self-pity into a tragic statement, to create a last role out of his existence after his profession has closed itself to him.

But it was Judy Garland, needless to say, who made the film unforgettable. Her's was an expert and extremely open performance, a performance that held back noth-

against the vindictiveness of a system bent on revenging itself for his past arrogances, made her performance all the more poignant.

At her best, in her mature years, Garland seemed always to be on the verge of breaking down in public (in fact, she did so at occasional personal appearances), and this charged her work with an infectious air of danger. It was seeing her reach the end of a performance intact that so often prompted orgies of emotion among the more impressionable of us.

She was, of course, a canny professional and by all accounts a woman sometimes capable of shrewd, tough, and humorous self-appraisal, so there was perhaps more art at work here than we thought. Having made us privy to so many of her problems, she knew perfectly well what would happen to an audience when–rather like Vicki Lester at the end of **A Star Is Born**–she pulled herself together and bravely, tremulously launched into the emotionally loaded "Over the Rainbow."

There were, of course, some who despised this confusing mixture of reality and artifice, deplored her play for ready sympathy. Yet there was an undeniable excitement about her, a sense that, like it or not, she showed us the brassy, childish, sentimental heart of show business. Not absolutely first class, you know; but perhaps it was the business' pretense of social concern, intellect, fineness of spirit–stuff she had no truck with–that was more profoundly false and misleading. Be that as it may, the fact remains that in 1954, objectively speaking–and sentimentally speaking– Garland deserved the Academy Award as best actress for her performance in **A Star Is Born.** That it went instead to cool and untroublesome Grace Kelly for **The Country Girl**–another show-bizzy story, but more deliberately sober in

ing–comically, romantically, melodramatically. She knew, and we knew she knew, just about everything there was to know about the price Hollywood could exact of its least stable, and therefore most emotionally vulnerable, performers. Indeed, this was but one of several comebacks–from unhappy marriages, from studio suspensions, from health problems–that made her career drama (along with Sinatra's and Elizabeth Taylor's) a singular part of "the business" during the fifties and sixties. The fact that in **A Star Is Born** she was playing not what she was in real life–a victim–but a heroine, a girl fighting stubbornly not only to develop her own career but to preserve her marriage and her husband's dignity against his own assaults on it, as well as its approach—says something about the true spirit of Hollywood, which thus paid Garland back for all the trouble she had caused it in the past. It was, indeed, the very spirit that the fictional Norman Maine encountered in the film. Nice irony there.

Rebel Without a Cause

1955

Marlon Brando came to the movies when he was twenty-five. James Dean was dead, **East of Eden** behind him, **Rebel Without a Cause** and **Giant** awaiting release, when he was twenty-four years old.

So much for the comparisons that sprang so readily to everyone's mind in 1955 and 1956, when Dean's life's work for the screen appeared. There really were none that could authentically be made. One man was, at the time, a major artist at the first peak of his career; the other was a phenomenon in search of a career. It might well have turned out to be an interesting one had he not lost his life in a motor accident, for James Dean had a lively, appealing instinct for his craft. He certainly cannot be blamed for the adolescent cult that began to grow up around him after his movie debut and reached Wertherian proportions after he died, when uncounted thousands of young people clung to the persistent rumor that he had survived his accident and was alive—though terribly maimed—in a nursing home somewhere or other. (Presumably, it was the same one that housed FDR, Glenn Miller, and other culture heroes whose deaths some people cannot bring themselves to accept.)

It is not difficult to see what they saw in Dean. Brando, for all the beatings he seemed to take pleasure in receiving in his films, was a much more powerful figure. Indeed, the reason he so often got clobbered was precisely because, on screen as well as off, he appeared such a dangerous menace to middle-class values and institutions. In none of his pictures did Dean menace anyone or anything. He was, in one way or another, always in flight. Pressed, he might stand and defend himself—successfully. (See the knife fight and the "chicken" race in **Rebel.**) Basically, however, adolescents saw in him and his problems projections of themselves and the things that troubled them.

Pauline Kael debatably sees more in him than that: "When the delinquent becomes the hero in our films, it is because the image of instinctive rebellion expresses something in many people that they don't dare

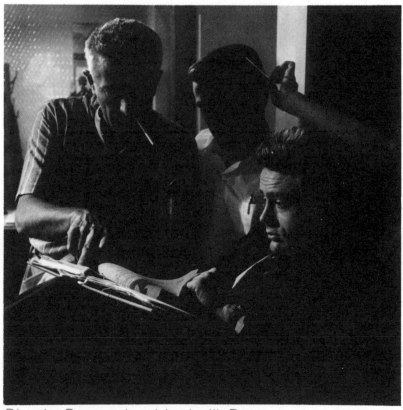

Director Ray and assistant with Dean.

express." It is probably a sound enough generalization, but it does not really apply to Dean's film persona, for though he expressed a certain unhappiness with his familial lot in both **Eden** and **Rebel,** in neither case did his response extend to overt or even covert criticism of society. The effort instead was to romanticize the child as victim. Dean himself was so seen—if only his father had stood up to his mother more manfully the boy might have been, we are given to understand, stronger, better able to defend himself against the world's impositions. More directly to this point in **Rebel,** however, was Plato, the character played by Sal Mineo. Rather small and intellectual for his age, he was the victim of parental neglect and, emotionally, very childlike. Above all, for all his brightness and charm, he was unworldly, innocent. Dean and his girl friend, played by Natalie Wood, first become his protectors and then, to all intents and purposes, his surrogate parents. The love and attention they lavish on him is exemplary. If only his parents, their parents, everyone's parents had been so kind, so understanding, none of the troubles afflicting them, and, by extension, the whole world, would have occurred.

How quickly our assumptions about the world change. Ten years later numbers of films and much more social commentary told us that youth was restive because its parents, far from neglecting them, had indulged them too much, given them too much materially (which was also an implication of fifties youth films). More important, they were given too much credit for moral and intellectual superiority—in short, "spoiled," to borrow an old-fashioned term now fallen into disuse.

Still, one thing is a constant: the youthfulness of movie audiences and the consequent necessity to cater to their romantic view of themselves as more sinned against than sinning, upholders of the good, the true, and the beautiful in a sold-out world. Dean, with his slight build, shy smile, and general air of sweet superiority—which no more than that other great culture hero of his historical moment, the fictional Holden Caulfield, could he satisfactorily explain or convincingly demonstrate—was the perfect repository for youth's unproved assumptions about itself.

His death, so far as one can determine the result of his own damnfoolishness—in any event, hardly the result of adult insensitivity or materialism or any of the other inequities he criticized simply by being present—did seem to prove a general point much treasured by adolescents: the good die young. And so he passed into legend—as did **Rebel Without a Cause,** the 1955 film which most tightly and clearly fitted his image. In general structure and attitudes it prefigured the "youth films" of a decade and more. And more than any other work it assured the reputation of its director, Nicholas Ray—a slick, competent craftsman of no special gift—because the film was so appealing, so influential on the first generation of academically recognized film students, many of them now full-scale Ph.D.-blessed "scholars" of the art. It hit them before they had chosen their profession, but they would not forget its creator. Nor, indeed, will its star be forgotten. His footnote in the social history of the fifties seems secure. All one wonders, remembering his native talent for acting, is whether he could have transcended his image, his cult, the prison being manufactured for him, and become an important and lasting star. Or would he, like so many bright-burning star phenomena, have become a burnt-out case, unable to shed light on the decades after the one he made his own.

Guys and Dolls

1955

Brando puts the squeeze on Joe.

At first, Brando didn't want to do the part. But then the director, Joseph L. Mankiewicz, sent him a cable: "UNDERSTAND YOU'RE APPREHENSIVE BECAUSE YOU'VE NEVER DONE MUSICAL COMEDY. YOU HAVE NOTHING REPEAT NOTHING TO WORRY ABOUT. BECAUSE NEITHER HAVE I. LOVE, JOE." Brando forthwith accepted the job.

One could wish that their collaboration on a second off-beat project–their first had been MGM's all-star **Julius Caesar**–had turned out as amusingly as it began. But, as was his custom, producer Samuel Goldwyn buried director and stars in a heavy, lavish production, and the verve and charm of Frank Loesser's songs emerged only fitfully from under this crushing weight. Still, as Mankiewicz (and Bob Willoughby) testify, they at least had some fun doing it, turning Brando into a song-and-dance man. And in retrospect that seems important, for Brando was not destined to have much fun with his career for almost two decades–until **The Godfather** and **Last Tango in Paris** turned out, at last, to be projects which were worthy of his enormous gifts.

The golden time for him was the beginning, from his debut in Zinnemann's **The Men** (1950) through his re-creation of his great stage performance as Stanley Kowalski in **A Streetcar Named Desire** and including his work in a series of films that remain memorable almost solely because of his presence: **Viva Zapata, The Wild One, On the Waterfront.** He had come warily to Hollywood, determined not to let the place wear him down or slick him up, as he felt it had done to so many promising young men before him. He had also arrived there arrogantly, sensing that the times were changing, that he personified a new mood among the younger members of the audience–an inwardness, if you will, which saw the important conflicts to be inside oneself, not necessarily with external forces. It must have seemed to him that Hollywood needed him perhaps more than he needed it. Therefore, he would have stardom on his own terms. Brando carried with him the hopes of the entire theatrical profession for a new deal. He was the first star produced by the so-called "Method," an adaptation of Stanislavski's techniques which, besides offering American actors freedom from their provincial thrall to the English style of playing, had a moral dimension as well. The adherents of The Method, conceiving themselves as embattled revolutionaries, were constantly critical of the commercialized theater, of show biz, ever watchful of threats to their integrity as artists. Brando, whether he liked it or not, was their champion– and their test case–on the West Coast. He was expected to undertake serious and important work there, expected to resist all assaults on his and–by extension–their integrity.

Stubborn, proud, ungrateful, he was at the start of his film career able to do work that satisfied him, the studios, his supporters in the profession, and the wider public. But he had a restless, if untutored, intelligence. He did not want to go on playing inarticulately rebellious young men. Character roles appealed to him especially, and so did comedy. In private life, intimate reports inform us, he has always been a superb mimic and a man of sly, self-mocking wit; he wanted to bring those aspects of his personality to bear on his art. Most important of all, he did not wish to be bored. Thus Sky Masterson, gambler and Broadway character, in **Guys and Dolls** represented an interesting challenge to him in 1955–if not, perhaps, to those who worried more than he did about the possibility of his "selling out." To his work on it he brought, according to Mankiewicz, quickness and sensitivity which made directing him an exciting experience and a challenging one, since he had an ability to ask the director the right questions when something went against his instincts or intuition.

So, if **Guys and Dolls** didn't quite come off (it went against the grain of Mankiewicz's talent, too, which is for a more brittle kind of comedy), it represented, for Brando, if not for his army of eager critics, a good and a sensible try to broaden his range. (Laurence Olivier has done this sort of thing throughout his career, to his own obvious delight and to that of his awed public, and it is curious that we have been so grudging in granting our approval to our best younger actor's attempts to do the same.)

Subsequently, Brando was not so fortunate in his attempts to stretch himself. **Sayonara** was junky on the whole, but a good vehicle for him. **One-Eyed Jacks,** his first and only attempt to direct himself, was beautiful to look at and a noble attempt to expand the western form. His performance in the remake of **Mutiny on the Bounty,** a masterpiece of characterization, was sabotaged by the studio, which resented his costly on-set rebellions when it reneged on various promises it had made to him about his role and the picture as a whole. There were flashes of fire in other doomed vehicles: **The Young Lions, Teahouse of the August Moon, The Ugly American.** But there was also a growing sense of desperation in his career, as he reached out for weird scripts like **Bedtime Story, The Night of the Following Day, Candy,** searching for material that would stimulate his imagination–even in the studios' slush piles. Everyone had pretty much written him off when he found a great character part in **The Godfather,** then followed it with **Last Tango,** in which he devastatingly showed his original Kowalski/**Wild One/Waterfront** rebel confronting the terrors of middle age.

Somehow, this last creation is more deeply satisfying than a mere "good performance" usually is. One gains from it a sense that Brando was communicating through his work just about everything he has learned, off-screen as well as on, about the pain of existence in the times we share with him. One has a sense of his rounding off, perhaps finishing, his professional life with a final, summarizing piece of workmanship.

It is impossible for anyone who came to maturity when Brando became a major figure in the celebrity drama of our time to speak objectively about him. If you were part of the so-called "silent generation," Brando was more than just an interesting star to you. For we were not, for the most part, silent out of fear. We were silent because we honestly did not know all–or perhaps any–of the answers. The old political and moral imperatives no longer appeared to be unquestionable and such new answers as the leaders and the self-appointed spokesmen of the fifties (and the sixties) offered did not appear to us so wonderful either. Brando became, for a lot of us, a symbol of our desire to speak about our anguish and our failure to do much more than half-articulate our displeasure with the way things were. When, in **The Wild One,** he is asked what he's rebelling against and he replies, "What have you got?" we heard issuing from the screen a voice we recognized–for all his highly individual mannerisms–as our own. Through Brando's many professional trials, beginning with the eagerness of comedians to parody him and ending with the crocodile tears of the show-biz establishment over his alleged failure to "fulfill his promise," a lot of us stuck with him, rooting for him. And those of us who did were amply rewarded–in **Last Tango**–by a summation of the conflicts and confusions of aging that was as accurate, and as moving, as his model characterizations of the conflicts and confusions of youth.

The Man With the Golden Arm

1956

Otto Preminger's many detractors insist that one of his great flaws is a lack of consistency. Ever since he set up shop as an independent producer-director in the early fifties, he has, they note, hopped blithely from subject to subject. Sex comedies, sex tragedies, musicals, mysteries, examinations of major social and political issues have issued from him in confusing profusion. Where–if anywhere–does his heart lie?

Wrong, say his defenders, mostly auteur critics. No matter what his sub-ject matter, there is consistency at least in his point of view. They speak of his "objectivity," his unwillingness to tip the scales of sympathy emphatically toward any particular character or point of view, even though the former may be the nominal hero of the enterprise, the latter its reason for existence. They find this quality even in his camera work and editing, where he prefers the two-shot to the close-up, eschews montage in favor of the long scene unbroken by changes of angle. Etc.

It is all very tiresome. There is, indeed, a consistency to his work, namely a garish vulgarity that begins with his choice of material. Whatever their subject matter, nearly all Preminger's films over the past couple of decades have been based on best-selling novels with highly publicizable slants to them and no literary merit whatsoever, extend to adaptations which broaden and/or flatten this material still further, and end in a directorial manner that is better described as cold, coarse, calculating, and cynical rather than as "objective."

Now, to be sure, it is a basic tenet of the auteur theory that a director's ability to impose a personal vision on a mechanistic and industrialized art form is a criterion of value–and there is some merit in the notion. On the other hand, too many of the theory's adherents tend to be content merely to find the personal statement in a medium that is too often impersonal; they never question the quality of the statement. Their overvaluation of Preminger's work is a perfect example of what can go wrong when the defense of a critical theory takes precedence over the critic's first duty, which is to keep his eye on the work at hand. The fact that the debate between the auteuristes and their opponents has been the liveliest issue in the critical press during the decades in which film criticism became a profession that young people aspired to, rather than a refuge for drunken rewrite men, says something, perhaps, about how much intellectual mileage we can get out of it.

But no matter. Preminger is, in his way, as typical of a troubled time in American film history as Stanley Kramer is in his. And, it must be said, his skill as a producer often has rescued him as a director. Whether he was casting Joseph Welch, the Boston lawyer and anti-McCarthy hero, as a judge in **Anatomy of a Murder,** or taking a chance on a fine young actor named George C. Scott in a pivotal character role in the same film, or asking Sir Laurence Olivier to play a detective in a murder mystery, he often achieved wonderful effects with his spasms of casting genius. Then, too, he seems to have a good deal of respect for talent, and therefore gives players he trusts freedom to dig into their roles, to do more with them than most directors do. Finally, his flare for publicity, both for himself and for his pictures, has made him a refreshingly old-fashioned, piratical figure on a movie scene that went increasingly gray during the fifties and sixties. He was fun to have around as the man you loved to hate, a man free of cant and pretense, stirring things up, a survival artist who has taken his lumps with urbanity and cheek.

And, it must be admitted that two or three of his films were successful as down-and-dirty entertainments—flashy, cheesy fun. One thinks of **Anatomy of a Murder, Ad-**

Kim and Otto.

vise and Consent, Bunny Lake Is Missing. Of his several attempts to be taken seriously, probably **The Man With the Golden Arm,** made in 1955, is the best. I don't want to see it again, you understand, and I don't remember it as vividly as I do some of Otto's gaudier clinkers, but it did pioneer the subject of drugs in the movies and it did demonstrate that Frank Sinatra, when interested, could sustain a long, central, difficult role. In particular, the harrowing sequence in which he quits heroin cold turkey remains a potent memory. I even thought that the adaptation of Nelson Algren's novel by Walter Newman and Lewis Meltzer did it a service. The novelist's overripe prose, a powerful and self-conscious barrier to sympathy with his people, was dispensed with, leaving the tough, realistic center of the story intact. Rather than romanticize drugs—as was done by the youthful drug culture of the late sixties—the film was unsparing when it came to showing the degradation of a junkie's life. It was good, too, in showing how dull-witted and inappropriate the institutions assigned to dealing with him were. For once—and only once—Preminger's search for sensational material led him to a place where the crudeness of his directorial sensibility was a strength, not a weakness. One sat up and paid attention to this film without knowing just how important its subject matter was about to become.

In short, there was some real feeling in the picture, even an air of compassion about it. And one wishes Preminger had found other projects in the years that followed which suited him as well as this one did. Somehow it enlisted him seriously rather than cynically. And it remains his one film which, whatever its imperfections—notably a rather dogged sobriety, a heaviness—can be respected for its aspirations and its more than partial fulfillment of them.

Raintree County

1956

Montgomery Clift was the third male star of the fifties who was widely alleged to sum up, in his person, the Zeitgeist of the decade. Alexander Walker, the excellent English critic, speaks of him reflecting "the anguished sensitivity" of the youthful audience of the time, acutely noting that he was a screen figure who seemed nearly always to be making a silent plea for protection. This was not always the case, of course. Early in his career—in **The Search,** in **Red River,** to some extent in **The Heiress**—he proved himself extremely capable of playing interesting variations, up-dated versions, of conventionally heroic screen figures.

But basically the generalization holds. More and more the flinch came to be something like a trademark with him, his confession that he only felt comfortable in the presence of children who could not exploit him or make insufferable demands on him rang painfully true. And then, as time passed, his roles came more and more to be those of victims (**A Place in the Sun**), passively tortured observers of other people's anguish (**I Confess, Miss Lonelyhearts,** and the title role in **Freud**), or merely peripheral characters (**The Misfits,** that doomed and dreary production). Walker again: "The hunching shoulders as if he were about to draw his head in like a tortoise to shelter in his shell; the voice that sounded parched from spiritual drought; the eyeballs popping out with the 'don't hit me' supplication; the impression of a man who has seen in daylight the sort of nightmares that other people only see when asleep: this was the later Clift who came to represent so

Waiting for sun in Raintree County.

well the man of concern cut off from others by his own impotence."

Raintree County, at the aesthetic level, may be the least significant film he made, at least until his last one, the posthumously released The Defector, which was little more than a "B" picture. At the time (1956), the conventional wisdom in the industry held that one good way to combat television was to offer audiences something they could not get at home, free of charge–namely, big pictures filled with thronging spectacle that could not be crammed onto the tiny screen and, indeed, was too expensive for any television producer to contemplate. It was not a bad theory and it worked occasionally during the fifties and sixties (Ben Hur, Lawrence of Arabia, Dr. Zhivago). The trouble was that when these multimillion-dollar productions flopped or ran hugely over budget (as any mighty production can), a studio could be left holding a giant bag, one so heavy that it could be dragged perilously close to bankruptcy. Raintree wasn't as big as the biggest of these disasters, but it was not, to begin with, a very promising idea. Based on the 1948 best seller by Ross Lockridge, the property had been on the shelf perhaps too long. It could not partake of the excitement an adaptation of a recent hit novel or play sometimes generates with the audience. Moreover, it was a kind of minor-league Gone With the Wind, full of antique passions, crinoline skirts, melodramatic personal disas-

ters, but suffering from an insufficiency of large-scale spectacle sequences of the sort that can make this kind of claptrap fun and memorable.

Worse, the disaster of his life and career happened to Clift while the film was shooting. He was involved in a near-fatal auto accident and required extensive plastic surgery on his face. As masculine features go, his had been almost beautiful, and though an expert job was done on him, the operations had the effect of freezing him in some subtle way. It also appears to have had some unknowable effect on his already delicate psyche. He became, henceforth, an even more haunted presence in his infrequent film appearances. The only thing he gained from this bad movie (which was directed, incidentally, by the ubiquitous Edward Dmytryk) was the lifelong friendship of his co-star, the powerful Elizabeth Taylor. She helped him obtain the role of the doctor opposite her in Suddenly, Last Summer and had him set for Reflections in a Golden Eye before trouble of some sort intervened and he rather mysteriously withdrew from the project.

Miss Taylor, of course, went on to tragedies of her own–brushes with death, the overblown "scandal" of her divorce from Eddie Fisher and her marriage to Richard Burton, supercelebrity. This had the effect of isolating her–as it so frequently does actors and actresses–from the main currents of her time and her art, turning her into a grotesque and even unconsciously self-parodying figure.

Indeed, in the histories of performers like Clift and Taylor one sees the hidden cost of Hollywood's changed way of doing business. Producing fewer, but generally more costly films, the studios desperately sought insurance for their scary investments. That meant they were willing to pay a great deal more to those few performers who seemed, often erroneously as it turned out, to guarantee a production's profitability. Such power gave actors and their agents a very large say in the shaping of a film (including cast and director approval, as well as approval of the script), but it also corrupted. The lack of constant work had a deleterious effect on the development of their talent. There came a time of revulsion, a cutback on large films, and (except for a very, very few) a deflation in the market for leading players. In the meantime an always chaotic and frightened industry grew even more so. The middle ground was cut from under it. Films were either big hits or large flops. There was no place for average, unpressured production, where actors could perfect their skills and, perhaps more important, through repeated exposure build a truly loyal following. (In the thirties and forties, a leading man or woman under studio contract might do three or four pictures in a year.) Similarly, directors and writers were denied a valuable proving ground for talents and ideas that might have slipped by in program features of earlier days.

The trouble with the Platinum Years is that there was entirely too much emphasis on platinum. The search for it led to a devaluation of honest sterling, sturdy stainless. Too often we discovered, when we got to the theater, that what we were seeing was merely platinum plate, an illusion nowhere near as satisfying as the humbler but more solidly crafted fare of earlier years. An accumulation of such experiences further diminished the habitual audience. More and more—like the moguls themselves—audiences held back, waiting for sure-fire stuff. What this new caution meant to the economics of the business, not to mention the art of the film, no one can accurately calculate. But it was terribly expensive.

Ocean's 11

1960

Ocean's 11 was the first formal aesthetic statement (to borrow a phrase that is preposterous in this context) of a phenomenon that everyone knew something about and was curious to know more about, namely that several members of show biz's elite of the moment—Frank Sinatra, Dean Martin, Sammy Davis, Jr., and Peter Lawford—had clubbed together, forming a nucleus around which an ever-changing population of other show folk congregated. Thus, **Ocean's 11,** though directed by the sober Lewis Milestone, was a triumph of the packager's art, for in the fifties and sixties the nation's interest in the hidden life of the celebrated had reached an historical peak. This film, which promised a more intimate view of them than the gossipists or the TV talk shows could provide, was a master commercial stroke in 1960.

It was set in the playpen most closely identified with them—Las Vegas—and it was about their attempt to break several banks at the casinos there, not by playing games of chance, but by launching a carefully timed set of heists. It was in some sense a precursor of a genre that was to become increasingly familiar and increasingly tedious as the decade wore on—the comedy caper. Most people, however, could not have cared less about the story as such. What the film promised, and to a degree delivered, was a portrait of "The Rat Pack" at play. (The title was adopted from a previous grouping of celebrities centered around Humphrey Bogart—who died in 1957—and known as "The Holmby Hills Rat Pack.") The trick in films like this, and in such successors as **Sergeants**

3, Convicts 4, Robin and the 7 Hoods, was to casually break out of the fictional frame, in the process allowing the thin masks of their characterizations to slip aside so the audience could share the ingroup's little jokes on one another. "Just kidding, folks," they seemed to say several dozen times a picture. We were, indeed, to understand that the group was such good friends that they couldn't bear to stay in character for the length of a sequence, let alone an entire film.

It is pointless to criticize them for lack of discipline or for printing and then releasing material that other stars would have insisted on burying. At its best their style could possibly be defended as having pioneered loose, improvisational comedy in a decade notable for the impoverishment of the comic muse. At its worst—which it generally was—the Rat Pack was, on screen, smug and contemptuous of its audience. And, as the decade wore on, no one was worse in this respect than Frank Sinatra. Occasionally he would pull himself together to sustain a character of some sort for the length of a picture, but these efforts were for the most part unappreciated. The same was true of Dean Martin. Both took to making quick, rip-off films in which careless charm was supposed to substitute for craft and distract us from their contempt for the paying customers, which was, in fact, a form of self-contempt. There is one anecdote that makes the point succinctly. While shooting a detective picture called **Tony Rome,** Sinatra was informed that the production was several days behind its shooting schedule. He casually selected a dozen or so pages from his script at random, yanked them out, threw them away, and said, "There—now we're on time."

Admittedly, Sinatra and the rest had larger fish to fry. Lawford at the time was married to Pat Kennedy, sister of John F. Kennedy, and they were—the lot of them—drawn into the political orbit. Actors and actresses had, of course, lent their names and presences to political activity in the past, just as they had, from time immemorial, taken and shaped roles to match their off-screen images. But, again, the Rat Pack took these traditions a step further. We were given to understand, erroneously or not, that this group was a good deal more intimate with the New Frontiersmen than show folk ordinarily were with their chosen candidates. In time, their roles, even as court jesters, were downgraded. There were always those rumors of Sinatra's mob connections to deal with, and then, too, the singer didn't always seem to know his place. He once called the venerable Sam Rayburn, Speaker of the House, "creep," and told him to take his hands off Sinatra's suit on the grounds that he was "bending it."

Inevitably, the Rat Pack

Veteran director Milestone eyes the scene.

broke up. Tragically, so did Camelot-on-the-Po-tomac. The former found themselves rallying to the support of politicians like Ronald Reagan, with Sinatra doing service above and beyond the call of duty as Spiro Agnew's friend and con-fidante. Indeed, the singer's famous loyalty to his friends even extended to raising money for the disgraced Vice President's legal defense fund after he was forced out of office. But perhaps the most pathetic sight of the post-Kennedy years was Sammy Davis, Jr. One recalls him on a talk show wearing a peace medallion, joking about his conversion to Judaism, and making the clenched-fist sign of the black militants; in short, trying everything he could think of to re-main "relevant." In the 1973 election campaign he was pictured publicly embracing Nixon.

If there is a moral in all this it is probably not that show-business celebrities should avoid entangling political alliances. It is impossible to prevent them from so doing and, anyway, it is their constitutional right. No, the main thing is not to take them seriously. After all, the modern celebrity game is their game. They invented it and it is the source of such power as they have. Politicians, McLuhanesque gurus, and all the rest are latecomers to it. They can, in their relative innocence, get mixed up about it, confusing personal notoriety with acceptance of the ideas and causes they espouse. Strolling players, on the other hand, have sense enough as a rule to stroll from one camp to another whenever the center of the ac-tion switches. Their attention to a given cause or leader is meaningless except as a measure of fashionability, and their defections are similarly unprincipled. They are merely a source of enter-tainment for the sophisticated observer—like everything else these creatures do to keep their place in the public eye.

My Fair Lady
1963

My Fair Lady was the theatrical success of the fifties. It opened on Broadway in the fall of 1955 and ran on into the next decade—more than three thousand performances in all. Around the world it has grossed well over $50 million from live performances alone. Jack Warner paid $5 mil-lion for the movie rights to the play and, in its turn, George Cukor's impeccable production re-leased in 1963 grossed $34 million, excluding its recent, very pricy sale to television. And the best part of it all is that its success tells us nothing at all about the sociocultural climate of either the fifties or the sixties—except that there is always an audience for tasteful, skillful, tune-ful, humorous entertainments. One imagines Lerner and Loewe's adaptation of Shaw's **Pyg-malion** would have been a success in the thir-ties or forties or, for that matter, in the seventies. Like many popular successes before and since, it awakened nostalgia for times suf-ficiently remote from the present to wash away the ugliness and awkwardness of reality in the golden glow of theatrical lighting. Unlike many other popular musicals of recent times, **My Fair Lady** made no pretense of dealing with social or existential issues, or of being particularly in-novative musically or theatrically. Its creators instead chose to work well within the es-tablished conventions of their genre, exploring and exploiting them to their limits. The result, then, was not a flawed but stimulating attempt to transcend those limits (like, say, **West Side Story**), but rather a work that summarized what had been best in the years since **Oklahoma!** ini-tiated the modern era of the musical theater.

Slick, graceful, light on its feet, **My Fair Lady** avoided the sometimes cloying folksiness of Rodgers and Hammerstein, the operatic pretensions of Frank Loesser and Leonard Bernstein. And George Cukor was the perfect director for it when it came time to transfer it to the screen. He had been a Broadway director before coming to Hollywood in 1930, one of the many stage directors recruited westward to help movies make the transition to sound, one of the few who stayed on happily and successfully. In his more than four decades in films, Cukor has acquired a deserved reputation as a subtle director of actors and a masterful adapter of sophisticated stage works in which he somehow managed to retain their essence, at the same time satisfying the often contradictory demands of the film medium. Like Lerner and Loewe, he accomplished this without ever seeming to breathe hard, although, unlike them, he has not been rewarded with enormous fame outside his own profession.

Anyway, Cukor is a man who respects generic conventions. He thinks they are not to be lightly cast aside or even toyed with very much. It is from them, he believes, that essentially lightweight works derive their tensile strength, a strength that can allow them to endure longer than many heavier, more ambitious works of the same vintage. His job, as a director, he has said, is to penetrate to "the reality beyond convention"–the basic human situations (as in the love that can bloom between a misogynistic male and a strong-willed woman) often found at the core of the most highly stylized works.

Hence the charm of his **Fair Lady.** He resisted the inevitable movieish pull toward realism. The film's exteriors powerfully suggest their familiar real-life models but avoid precise duplication. The moviegoer's eye has

Cukor in his Fair Lady's chair.

been trained to demand a higher degree of authenticity in these matters than the stage spectator needs or wants, and the film satisfies this demand. At the same time the sets subtly suggest the artificer's hand, reminding us at every turn that this is a theatrical piece, not life as it is, but as it ought to be. The film's Covent Garden is so much more attractive than London's, for example. Its Ascot—with the horses blurring by, colorful shadows rather than several tons of three-dimensional horseflesh—is a little masterpiece of artificiality. But throughout, the temptation to "open it up"—as the saying in the movies goes—has been resisted. Basically the play takes place in interior sets, the continuing miracle of it being that so much life can be introduced in Edwardian parlors without a sense of crowding. Thus, if memory serves, no scenes that took place inside a home in the stage play were reset outdoors in order to impart a false sense of movement or splendor for the camera's sake. It moves about quietly, a perfect gentleman about not calling attention to itself, within these tight confines. A few new bits of business were invented for the film—notably a wonderfully steamy bath in which Prof. 'iggens' female staff cleanses the accumulated dirt of the street off Eliza Doolittle. It is humorous, cinematic, and in no way jars our expectations of a beloved and familiar work—one which we would not wish to see tampered with by movie people.

In short, the film had the lavishness which audiences had come to expect of major productions during the Platinum Years, but it was a tasteful lavishness which did not weigh down the production. Cukor has since confessed that he did not get on well with Cecil Beaton, employed to translate his production designs from stage to screen, indicating that his own long-standing team of designers contrib-uted as much or more to the finished work than did the highly publicized Englishman. Be that as it may, the film turned out to be one of the few aesthetically satisfying screen adaptations of a Broadway success, almost making one forget a truly regrettable tendency of the period—Hollywood's virtual halt in creating original musicals specifically for the movie medium. (Which happened, ironically, just when it was getting good at it—**Seven Brides for Seven Brothers, Singin' in the Rain, The Bandwagon.**) The film won the Academy Award for best picture of the year, plus all kinds of other Oscars for everything from best actor to best sound recording. Among them was one for George Cukor as best director—a prize he might logically have won at least a dozen times previously.

Marnie

1964

The late fifties and early sixties were, among other things, the great age of Alfred Hitchcock's art. There is no valid sociological reason for this, though in an apolitical period, when individuals were self-absorbedly picking away at their psyches as if they were so many scabs, it is not surprising that most of his psychologically disturbing films found great favor with the public. As for the great director himself, the wry, sly, appealing but rather slight English period (**The 39 Steps, The Lady Vanishes**) was well behind him, and so was the Selznick period when the producer's heavy-thumbed taste for expensive decor and slow-moving romance warred with Hitch's essentially nimble, technically adroit, and elegant technique. Functioning now as his

own producer he turned out a succession of films that sacrificed nothing in quickness while exploring with greater depth those pathological quirks–the guilts, compulsions, obsessions, and fetishes–that had always preoccupied him profoundly. **Rear Window, To Catch a Thief, The Wrong Man, Vertigo, North by Northwest, Psycho, The Birds**–these were his mature masterpieces, and if **Marnie** is not quite up to them it is still a most interesting and revealing film.

The title character–uninterestingly played by the least gifted of Hitchcock's many cool blondes, Tippi Hedren–is a compulsive thief. Her illness, which has its roots in a violent incident of her childhood, is discovered by an employer (extremely well played by Sean Connery) who has his own compulsions. One is a powerful masculine need to prove himself sexually by acting as the instrument of this frigid woman's sexual awakening. The other is a fetishistic desire to make it with a cripple, albeit a psychological cripple. In short, sickness matches sickness; the film is a prime example of the basic neurotic relationship which we have lately taken to calling, in R. D. Laing's phrase, "a double bind."

The suspense in the film at first arises out of the fact that we, the audience, know that Marnie must steal and wonder how long she will resist the temptation. When she finally does succumb, her theft from the office safe is handled with Hitchcock's customary mastery of simple suspense-film technique. But what really gives us the creepy-crawlies is not this criminal activity, but the claustrophobic situation to which it leads. To prevent exposure as a thief Marnie must marry the boss, to whom she refuses to yield either on her wedding night or on any subsequent night. Checkmate. And worse, for the possibility grows more likely by the day that one of her previous victims may recognize her and reveal not only her shame but embarrass the great family into which she has married (social degradation, the wealthy and the respectable dragged before the bar of justice like common criminals, is perhaps the most recurrent of all Hitchcock's themes). What saves her and, indeed, saves the picture, which is rather cold and clinical a good part of the way, is Connery's growing sympathy for his prisoner, the realization that she is caught in the toils of an ancient trauma which she has blocked from consciousness and which he must help her to rediscover and confront before she can achieve something like normality. This sympathy turns to something like love and that love more or less cancels out the ugly motives which led him into the relationship.

The blocked incident turns out to be, finally, rather melodramatic and unpersuasive. Even Hitchcock has since conceded that it is no more than a dramatic convention, a way of satisfying our need for a happy resolution for this situation. He has said he does not think his lovers will live happily ever after. But then, he was born a Catholic and he believes more profoundly in original sin than he does in happy endings. Indeed, in Hitchcock's universe it nearly always turns out that everyone is guilty of something, though that something may not–usually is not–the crime for which the police seek him or for which he is put on trial. "The wrong man" (or woman) usually turns out in some sense to be the right man, a guilty party of some kind. It is this all-encompassing moral disapproval, this sense that everyone is fallen, far more than the suspense generated by chase or mystery that makes his films so edgy, so much more disturbing and memorable than the usual exercises in cinematic suspense. In the age of anxiety he is the movies' great artist of anxiety and, come to think of it, it may be no accident that he was inspired to his greatest heights, and found his most eager audience, in the late fifties and early sixties, when the national mood was a vaguely troubled one, when we could not quite isolate and articulate the way we can today what was bothering us, but knew, as in a dream, that something was not quite right, that we were guilty in one way or another of sins of omission, if not of commission.

The Great Race

1965

The Great Race was in some ways as typical of its period (1965) as any movie you can think of. The intention was reasonable enough–to recapture the innocent merriment of silent comedy for modern audiences. The picture was dedicated "To Mr. Laurel and Mr. Hardy," and it was one long–very long–'round-the-world chase in which two rival daredevils (Tony Curtis dressed in the pure white of goodness, Jack Lemmon in evil black with cape and villain's mustache) pursued one another and a large cash prize offered by a newspaper to whomever could most quickly circumnavigate the globe. Natalie Wood was the girl reporter covering the event. As they arrived in various exotic quarters, the director, Blake Edwards, was able quite easily and naturally to work in satires of old-time movie genres: a sheik romance, a mad-scientist thriller, a submarine adventure, a western, a Ruritanian romance. He even managed to get his principals into a pie shop, so he could recreate a custard-pie throwing sequence widely advertised as the biggest ever attempted in Hollywood.

The conception was attractive enough, but the execution was something else again. What everyone forgot–or chose not to remember–was that the essence of silent comedies was their poverty. They represented (and herein lies their timeless appeal) the triumph of invention over the limits of minuscule budgets and primitive technology. They often looked as if they had been shot in vacant lots. They were nearly always made on very short shooting schedules and without detailed scripts. The director usually sallied forth with no more than an outline of the overall plot and the description of some gags sketched out by the gagmen. There was, of necessity, a good deal of improvisation on the set (or perhaps in the nearest bar during a lunch break), which accounts both for their moments of divine inspiration and for their sudden, unaccountable lapses from grace. In any event, their cheapness accounted for their enormous profitability (Harold Lloyd would have been a millionaire if he had made nothing but one of his least-remembered hits, **Grandma's Boy)** and their surrealist charm. For a silent comic–usually a rather odd-looking fellow to begin

with—was always getting into these extraordinary situations just by walking down some ordinary, familiar-feeling street, doing something as banal as walking into a shop to buy some staple product or entering a restaurant for dinner—just as any member of his audience had done a thousand times. The result was, of course, as weird and frantic as one of those dreams in which we find ourselves walking down a street unclothed or inching along a skyscraper's ledge.

The Great Race had none of the flaky qualities of the films to which it was supposed to be paying tribute. Director Edwards is a gifted entertainer (**Breakfast at Tiffany's,**

The Party, etc.) who also happens to be a painstaking workman, notorious for bringing his pictures in astronomically over budget; in short, a man of cautious calculation rather than of sudden inspiration. Which is to say that no matter how profound his desire to pay his predecessors the sincerest form of flattery, his natural gift went against the grain of the enterprise.

Perhaps more important, so did the spirit of the time. The last era in which the comic muse functioned with any degree of regularity in American movies was the thirties—the Marx Brothers, W. C. Fields, Mae West, the screwball comedies of Howard Hawks, Leo Mc-

Carey, et al. The forties, excepting the exceptional Preston Sturges, had been a dim time, the fifties a hopeless one, the sixties the dreariest of them all. Nothing seemed very funny at the moment and, anyway, Hollywood's tendency to overdress and overproduce just about anything gave its increasingly rare attempts at comedy a terrible weight handicap—especially considering that these films were supposed to run a much longer distance than earlier features. (A silent comedy was rarely more than an hour long; the sound comedies of the thirties rarely stretched as long as ninety minutes.) **The Great Race** had a running time of something like two hours, and its cost was an unbelievable $12 million. Charles Chaplin's lifetime output was financed for a good deal less.

Perhaps no genre showed the weakness of the industry's Standard Operating Procedures from the mid-fifties to the mid-sixties more clearly than comedy. Huge outlays on a single film are always a risky gamble, but creating a **Lawrence of Arabia** or a **Dr. Zhivago** (to name a couple of good bets), or a **Cleopatra** (to name a very bad one), gives one no choice. Either one was willing to spend or one did not begin the project. And aesthetically, in a few cases, like **Lawrence,** the film's satisfactions were in part a direct result of the producer's willingness to spend money in order to show us wonders we had not beheld before.

But comedy? Excepting perhaps **Dr. Strangelove** (which wasn't all that expensive), it is impossible to name a good one that was also costly. The essence of the art is its lightness afoot, its quickness. However worthy the director or appealing the stars, those qualities are vitiated by huge casts or production values that distract from—and often bury—the jokes. Or to put it simply, there is more humor in one

perfectly thrown custard pie than in a thousand carelessly thrown ones. It is only an affluent society that entertains—and attempts to entertain itself with—the notion that it can simply spend its way into a good, humorous mood. More often than not, the sight of such excesses as history's biggest pie fight attracts only the lowest levels of curiosity, then begins to sicken us with its waste and stupidity. **The Great Race** was almost a paradigm of American society at its time. It was affable, good-natured, by no stretch of the imagination mean-spirited or intentionally evil. But, like that society, it was slow in its reactions, rather crass and insensitive (even about the things it set out to honor), and on the whole more stupid than it had to be. In comedy, as in life itself, there was no need to offer us platinum. Most of us would have settled for a less precious metal. It was just that no one seemed too interested in selling that other stuff anymore.

Who's Afraid of Virginia Woolf? brought together four of the great cultural–or were they merely publicity?–phenomena of the sixties: Edward Albee, the playwright for a time regarded as the American theater's most promising young writer; Mike Nichols, making his debut as a film director after an admirable career as a performer (with Elaine May in improvisatory comedy sketches) and as a director of light comedy on Broadway; and, of course, Elizabeth Taylor and Richard Burton, making their only worthwhile appearance together after their marriage, with its attendant titillations which had inevitably turned them into a star team (**The VIPs, The Sand-piper,** ad nauseam).

It is perhaps a measure of the American theater's desperate need for a first-class playwright that it could seize the standard falling from the tired grasp of such would-be titans as Tennessee Williams and Arthur Miller and prematurely welcome Albee, who had done a couple of minor, interesting things off-Broadway, as a major artist on the basis of this effort. **Virginia Woolf** is, at best, a high-class situation comedy with some absurdist overtones tacked on none too subtly. All that happens is that a couple of faculty couples at an apparently undistinguished New England college get together for an evening of boozing and truth-telling. The husband of the older pair reveals his weakness and (literal) impotence; she reveals that the child who occupies much of her conversation is a fantasy developed to make her disappointed life bearable. In the end, it is revealed that something akin to love–actually it's more of a double bind, as R. D. Laing would shortly be calling it; a neurotic knot–exists between them.

All of this, however, was no more than a strained convention, an excuse permitting Albee to do what he does (or did) best: write excruciatingly tough and funny duets and arias for actors, eminently playable scenes that didn't mean much, but were as entertaining to listen to as anything the American theater offered then, sort of super-Neil Simon stuff.

And Burton and Taylor played it well. Each has a vocal curse. His is a tendency to excessively classy speech; he sometimes seems to narrate rather than act a part. But **Look Back in Anger** (which he finally got to play in the movies) was written for him, because he has–or had–a powerful sense of outrage. And **Virginia Woolf** gave him an opportunity to vent that side of his personality. It also gave him an opportunity to demonstrate a capacity for self-pity, even weakness, that his more heroic characterizations in more routine films did not afford him. As for Miss Taylor, her least attractive attribute is a shrill and unmodulated voice, which she has never troubled to train. Here, as a shrew, this weakness was, in fact, strength.

As for Nichols, **Virginia Woolf** remains the only movie he has ever made in which the text was widely regarded as sacred. He was free to do the thing he does best–invent stage business for his players. He did not have unquestioned creative dominance here; that belonged to the play itself. Therefore, he could not muck it up with the shallow, radical-chic misanthropy that has marred all his later work for the screen. He was also intelligent enough to understand that this was one play that could only be hurt by "opening it up." Better by far to take the route Hitchcock had explored in some of his best works, keeping the work confined, claustrophobic to the point of suffocation. Aided immeasurably by Haskell Wexler's Academy Award-winning black-and-white photography, he seemed to burrow into the play, making it a more intense emotional experience than it had been on the stage. It seemed we were with these people for the entire, gritty length of their endless Saturday night, gnawing at each other's vitals.

At the time, of course– 1966–**Virginia Woolf** was a test case for the adult screen. Would the keepers of the motion-picture code allow Albee's celebrated strong language to go forth onto screens that, just an historical wink ago, belonged to the very different family of Judge Hardy? If they did, what would be the response of church groups and the freelance moralists? They did and–to paraphrase a line from an earlier battle for cinematic free

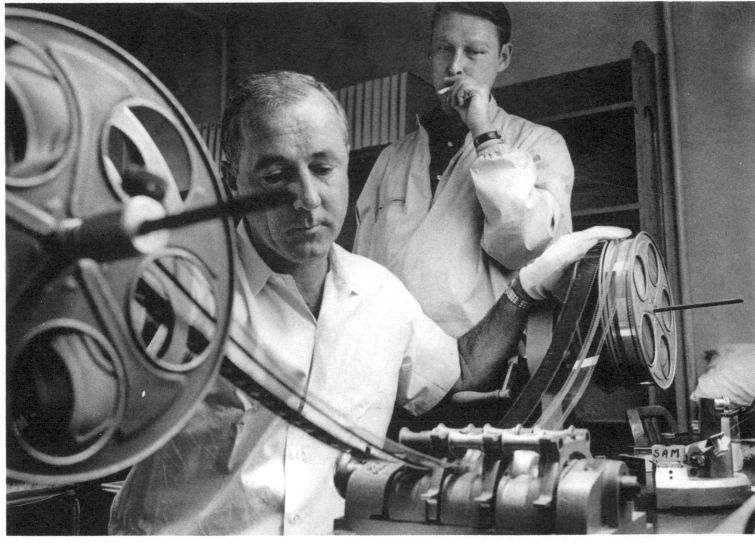

speech–frankly, my dear, no one gave a damn. The picture turned out to be a critical and commercial success.

And for the majority of its participants it was a high-water mark. Albee never achieved the continuing success everyone predicted for him–perhaps precisely because everyone had predicted it for him. He was last heard from publicly trying to heckle Eugene McCarthy from the floor at a New York political gathering. The defeated presidential candidate silenced him by telling the playwright he never had been able to write a third act and that he, McCarthy, was not about to provide one for him.

Taylor and Burton wrapped themselves more and more tightly in a cocoon which could only be penetrated by yes-men bearing projects ranging from the grotesque to the ghastly. Victims of their own celebrity, they had become, by the early seventies, self-parodies. Nichols, of course, went on to direct one of the decade's most successful and influential films, **The Graduate,** but he too declined as a creative force–in inverse proportion to the amount of creative control he was permitted to exercise over his films. Inevitably, we shall encounter him again. But unlike Albee, Burton, and Taylor, there will be no temptation to feel sorry for him.

A Man for All Seasons

1966

A Man for All Seasons was the quintessential mid-cult drama of its decade. Dwight Mac-Donald pioneered the use and definition of this neologism, and what it comes down to–in the theater and movies, anyway–is a discussion, in high-flown language, of some conveniently abstract issue such as the nature of truth or justice or loyalty, or something like that, between characters swathed in historical costumes and surrounded by scenery that somehow suggests the timelessness of these matters. If the characters batting this material back and forth can be important historical, or perhaps even mythic, personages, that's good, too. For besides getting "provocative" debate the audience is also pro-

vided with bits of historical and cultural information which is ever so helpful in brightening their conversation. They are also wonderfully comforted to know that significant people long ago fretted over the same issues that bother us today; it helps modern man to link himself to a great tradition.

Robert Bolt's successful play about Sir (later Saint) Thomas More and that nasty bit of business he had with Henry VIII was a perfect vehicle for middle-class discussion groups. More was, after all, someone with whom the contemporary technocrat could identify: a poor lad who had grown up to be not only the good head of a numerous and prosperous bourgeois family but the king's theological consultant, as well–a sort of reader-adviser in the monarch's bickerings with the Church of Rome. It was thus easy for the modern corporate manager (or lawyer or tax man or whatever) to identify with him, since they had, many of them, similarly placed their good brains in the service of less good ones who happened to have power. In time, of course, His Majesty required a rationale for a divorce which, as we know, More, in a spasm of conscience, refused to provide him. After many a wordy disquisition on the question of church-state relations, much phumpheting over where loyalty to the one ends and the other begins, and a modest amount of drama over whether it was worthwhile to lay one's head on the block over such matters, More, in the play as in history, goes to his doom.

One heard, in the pleased babble of the lobby after both the play and Fred Zinnemann's film adaptation of it, that many an easy and flattering identification with Paul Scofield's hero had been made. The American corporate underling—the organization man, the pyramid climber so much discussed in the nonfiction of the fifties and sixties—had often been in a position analogous to More's. He had often had difficulty squaring the demands of conscience with the demands of the job, had experienced the loneliness and discomfort More felt. And such people liked to believe that, like him, they might have compromised on small points, but that if the issue were something more than, say, a squabble over marketing strategy, if the dispute had a moral dimension, they would willingly risk if not life than life-style rather than truckle to the boss.

Thus the care and feeding of popular fantasies in the movies of this period. And, alas, this was a fantasy. For as the conglomerators gathered force in the sixties, we saw how desperately the org man scrambled to retain his corner office after the merger. We read in the business publications compassionate articles advising him how to handle threats to his status

posed by the new—and often morally very slippery—ways of doing business. Scandals—ranging from price-fixing among the functionaries of the giant electrical manufacturers to General Motors' harrassment of its critics to ITT's attempts to settle the antitrust case against it not only out of court but out of sight as well—proved that there were no Thomas Mores lurking in our executive suites.

The movie was, like all Zinnemann's work, handsomely photographed, a succession of gorgeous still photographs; but it cannot be said that this spoonful of visual sugar really helped the medicine go down. It did not, for instance, hasten the stately pace of the film. There is a convention that when seriousness strikes an American film maker, he must slow things down, perhaps because being unfamiliar with the process personally, he labors under the delusion that the formation and articulation of abstract ideas is of necessity a ponderous process. One also observes in films of this type a possibly unconscious feeling on the part of their makers that something as high-toned as **A Man for All Seasons** cannot possibly be appreciated unless the audience suffers a degree of pain, for has it not been written that culture does not come easily? Has it not been bred into the American bones that something that is good for you must of necessity subject one not to the sharp but possibly stimulating discomfort of offensiveness, but to the dull ache of boredom?

No matter, perhaps. **A Man for All Seasons** was a commercial success and was named best picture of the year by the motion picture Academy, with Zinnemann winning the Oscar for direction and Paul Scofield winning the statuette as the year's best actor—his diction being everyone's dream of classiness. One is, of course, offended by the ease with which not only the industry but also the public in general is taken in by works that are stiff with cultural aspiration. On the other hand, one is not surprised —at least one feels one should not be surprised— when awards go to films of this sort. The best American films—those quick, energetic, delightful comedies and action films which have been the glory of our cinema from the beginning—are rarely nominated, let alone given prizes either by Hollywood or by the various critics' groups which annually bestow awards on movies and movie makers. We have always, for some reason, aspired to make the movies something they are not naturally and probably never should be, namely, high cultural experiences. We show our true feelings unceremoniously, by running and rerunning on television and in the revival houses the works of Howard Hawks and Raoul Walsh and the other native masters of the unpretentious film forms, while **A Man for All Seasons** and such uplifting predecessors as **Wuthering Heights** and **Mrs. Miniver** and **The Best Years of Our Lives** languish on the shelves, half-forgotten souvenirs of brief, past enthusiasms for what seemed at the moment the highest of ideals one should aspire to.

Dr. Dolittle

1967

In 1964 Walt Disney Productions released **Mary Poppins.** To date it has returned $40 million to its distributors. A year later Twentieth Century-Fox released **The Sound of Music.** As of the end of 1973 it had grossed $83 million—more than any other film in human history with the notable exception of that impressive late starter, **The Godfather.** As a result of these successes it was borne in on Hollywood that there was a market out there for films to which the whole family might safely and merrily repair.

This was scarcely news. At least it shouldn't have been. For the ability to provide a steady flow of films—nearly all of which were individually capable of simultaneously pleasing most of the subgroups comprising the great habitual audience for movies—had been the basic condition of the industry's financial success prior to the advent of television. What was pleasing to its new leaders was the discovery that such films were still capable of luring Mom, Pop, and all the kids away from the tiny screen and back into the theaters. Of course, **Poppins** and **Music** were carefully differentiated from family entertainment, TV-style. They were musicals, naturally, a form rarely attempted by television. More than that, they were period musicals, with a lavish emphasis on the manners, costumes, and decor of times and places that were both interestingly exotic and, it seemed, more graceful than our own time and place. It cannot be said that either of these films was inimitable. On the contrary, the formula appeared to be easily imitable and a ready source of new profits.

Hence, **Dr. Dolittle.** It looked like it had everything. Based on a series of children's books beloved by several generations, it starred the **My Fair Lady** man, Rex Harrison, in another role in which he could easily exert his cranky charm. The period—nineteenth-century England—lent itself to recreation as something both handsome and nostalgic while the story—about a peculiarly gifted veterinarian who could talk to his patients and compare their excellent characters very favorably indeed to those of his human acquaintances—had a distinct appeal. Moreover, as a highly stylized, unrealistic work it was very suitable for the interpolation of songs and dances, which turned out to be very pleasantly managed.

But something went wrong. Like the very similar **Chitty-Chitty Bang-Bang** made around the same time, **Dr. Dolittle** proved to be a dismal flop. What's puzzling is why. It was not appreciably worse than its predecessors. Indeed, to the degree that it was less sugary than **Sound of Music** it was that much better. To the degree that its score was musically and lyrically more sophisticated than that of the Disney film, it was better than **Poppins.** Was the market for this kind of material that much smaller than anyone realized, capable of absorbing only a couple of these extravaganzas per decade? Was there a fundamental shift in the national mood between 1965, when **The Sound of Music** opened, and 1967, when **Dr. Dolittle** appeared? Certainly such optimism as had survived the Kennedy years was being rapidly dissipated by the crisis in confidence created by the Vietnam nightmare; but politico-social analysis of the factors affecting a film's box-office performance is rarely persuasive, there being too many exceptions to any generalization you care to make about the whys and wherefores.

I have the feeling that for once the critical reception of the picture, which normally has little effect on films engineered for the family trade, had something to do with this particular failure. That response was uncommonly harsh. It was as if a lot of critics, having indulged the sentimentalities of its predecessors perhaps too willingly, decided to prove their devotion to the finer things by kicking **Dolittle** around. Such considerations, semiconscious, half-formed, do enter the evaluative process, even when one is doing his best to guard against them. Anyway, the picture was stomped harder

Bovine extra waits patiently.

than was strictly necessary and it did not recoup its producers' investment. Yet, if it was not in any absolute sense good, it was also not bad by the standards we ordinarily apply to light entertainment. One would have wished, again, that its makers had pondered the famous dictum that less is more, that in contemplating the possibilities for family entertainment they had considered the notion that the family could conceivably be amused by something other than a nostalgic musical. Still, given the conventions of the moment and given the pleasure of Rex Harrison's company, not to mention that of a Pushmi-pullyu, and of a giant pink sea snail capable of transporting his entire party around the South Seas, and of the huge, jolly menagerie here assembled, **Dr. Dolittle** was not without its modest merits. Indeed, in the middle of the sixties one recalls there were a great many more tediously wasted hours than the couple a relative handful of us devoted to this well-meaning film.

The Graduate

1967

Is there anything left to say about **The Graduate**? It was probably the most significant film of the late sixties, the picture which pioneered the so-called "youth market," causing dozens of producers to believe that if they, too, catered to young people's flattering self-image as romantic rebels, they might also realize something like the $50 million gross Joseph E. Levine took in on Mike Nichols' film. That most of them did not says something about the volatility and the self-absorption of this audience: Their attention span was minute and their love of themselves so intense that there was room in their hearts for only one or two films about themselves, however flattering. And anyway, how could crass, old Hollywood possibly capture their sublime spirit, the greatness of their generation's soul?

It is impossible to deny that **The Graduate**—at first humorously, then its later portions seriously (if less successfully) —caught and held for us the restive mood of "the kids," as their professorial and media apologists and fellow travellers insisted on calling them. Their impatience with "plastics," their disappointment over the national discovery that money could not buy happiness, their gathering sense of impatience (and impotence) as the great corporate-government-educational machine clanked mindlessly onward, grinding down individuality and even the illusion that the citizenry could shape the policies and actions of their society humanely, was deftly suggested by the film in a cheerfully palatable manner. Dustin Hoffman's performance in the title role was expertly engaging and Nichols' direction was, for the most part, ingratiating and inventive: Hoffman trying out his graduation present (a scuba-diving suit) in his family swimming pool while a party swirls heedlessly about him; or his hilarious attempt to cool his way through a hotel-room assignation with an older woman who just happens to be the mother of his girl friend. One couldn't help but feel a certain sympathy for a young man engaged so amusingly in the tradi-tional task of "finding himself" in a world where the adults were less than usually helpful, having either botched the job themselves or never hav-ing bothered to undertake it.

Even so, there was something irritating about the film. It never explored or explained just what its hero had ac-complished to feel he had earned the right to crit-icize his elders. One hates to sound like those vulgarians who enjoy pointing out that social critics have never had to meet a payroll, but it is also true that the rebellious youth of the sixties never had to meet any of the ambiguous anxie-ties of adult responsibility either, raising de-fenses against the exactions of job-holding, family life, citizenship—all of which are more dif-ficult and contain more hidden traps than are readily obvious to the idealistic young bystander. Thus, though he's attractive in his sweet beffud-dlement, **The Graduate** is also something of a pain in the ass.

And the ending of the film, in which he rescues his girl from the very altar where she was about to marry a particularly awful example of the fraternity-man type is un-persuasive. We don't really believe this con-fused, ambivalent young man could suddenly pull himself together and swoop down upon a problem in so decisive a fashion. Nor do we real-ly believe that his victims—the families of the couples about to be married—would let him get

Director Mike Nichols.

away with it. Perhaps they would not, in reality, have given chase to the bus which is the escape vehicle into which he bundles his love (having briefly forestalled pursuit by jamming the church's door with a heavily symbolic cross). But surely annulment and other legal maneuvers would have pursued the couple for an unpleasantly long time to come.

All right, we are perhaps being too literal. **The Graduate** is just a fairy tale, after all. But the men who made it demonstrated in their other works and in the early portions of this one, that they had it in them to satirize youth's pretentions to moral superiority. And we know that such satire could have had a healthy, purgative effect on the audience for this film, which incidentally included a great many adults lured out to see it because their offspring convinced them that it, better than any other source (including themselves), would explain the mysterious younger generation to the puzzled, troubled oldsters. That, in the end, it sold out to the inflated and hypocritical self-image of the people it should have been satirizing made **The Graduate** appear to be a peculiarly cynical and contradictory enterprise.

Of course, one can never blame movie makers for trying to make a buck. It's an attitude that goes with the territory. But one is entitled to view with some concern the ease with which critics and the intelligent audience allowed them to get away with it in this instance. There were serious issues at stake here. Our consolation perhaps is that, like other excrescences of historical moments (Charles Reich's **The Greening of America,** for example), it has no historical resonance except as an example of the kind of fad that periodically sweeps through popular culture and creates a mania, the Kung Fu of its day.

Petulia

1968

Petulia was a near-perfect summary of both the style and the attitudes prominently featured in movies aspiring to a chic repute in the sixties. That style may be described as an attempt to approximate, on screen, a neurotic's stream of consciousness: the nervously zooming camera repeatedly fastens on bits of decor and landscape that a more sanguine sensibility would have ignored, but which seem to symbolize for middle-class miserables everything that is tawdry, graceless, and excessively materialistic about their world; jump-cutting is employed because attention spans are short and minds are cluttered like attics with the strange junk imparted by the unceasingly informative media; time-sequences are jumbled because the world seems to many of us incoherent, virtually without rational structure.

Style indirectly revealed much about the attitudes underlying this tale of a doctor who falls in love with a self-consciously kooky younger woman while both are in the process of separating themselves from their spouses (who are seen to be even less stable—and far less attractive—than these central figures). But just to make it clear, the picture insisted on the impossibility of genuine emotional engagement in a world of topless restaurants, automated hotel hospitality, and television sets braying the bad news from Vietnam unattended in the corner of the living room.

The strange thing about **Petulia** was that it worked, perhaps better than any other work of American social criticism one can recall from this period. In part that was due

to George C. Scott's authoritative, ruefully humorous portrayal of a man nearly immobilized by despair, incapable finally of finding the nerve to take on full-time responsibility for the title character. In part it was due to the febrile force Julie Christie brought to that role. She was here, as elsewhere, extraordinarily effective at suggesting the distorting effects of our times on the feminine psyche—the role-playing forced on women by insecurity, the abuses suffered in a society less aware than it is now of its sexism.

Mostly, however, the film's success—which was not a commercial one, nor by any means a unanimous critical one—belonged to Richard Lester. An American who had worked in British television, he had achieved his first widespread acclaim for **A Hard Day's Night,** the Beatles' first theatrical feature, a wackily engaging bit of throwaway expressionism. He did a less good sequel, **Help!,** an oddly flat adaptation of the stage musical, **A Funny Thing Happened on the Way to the Forum,** and a disasterous antiwar tract, **How I Won the War,** full of show-biz intellectuality, at once pretentious and offensive, as if he were trying to drive away his audience. In **Petulia,** however, he demonstrated an ability to delicately control his material, to give us characters with a certain depth and roundedness.

Reviewing the movie when it was released, I wrote: "Petulia and friend are nice enough to identify with, but they are not, finally, so charming or delightful that you feel like indulging them to excess. Each has a hard core of selfishness and foolishness that cannot be washed out; they contain within themselves the very qualities against which they are in rebellion—how could they not, since they, too, are the creatures of their era? Their tragedy is that unlike the majority of their fellow sufferers, they are aware of what's happening to them. They are not the blind bourgeoisie of **The Graduate,** they do not need an insufferably superior adolescent to show them what's wrong with them. They know, they know—and still they can't quite make it to decency and repose."

This painful self-awareness, an awareness leading to a kind of emotional stasis, in which people understand that all the alternatives to their present pain involve the acceptance of other kinds of pain and therefore do nothing was (and remains) a convention of existential fiction, but it was anticinematic. We prefer some kind of more positive resolution in films, even if it involves the kind of falsity that climaxed **The Graduate,** and that surely conditioned **Petulia's** commercial failure. So, too, I

Cold light on Richard Lester.

believe, did Lester's choice of a setting. San Francisco has gained the reputation of being America's Heavenly City, a civilized, human-scale urban area which belies the conventional wisdom that all our metropolises are impossible. For Lester to show that the Bay Area was as ugly and unpleasant as anywhere else—as alienating—was a form of lese majesty resented by the middle-brow audience which clings to its illusions as hard as the old mass audience did.

And so a modestly truthful film, a film that intelligently deployed the new conventions of the commercial cinema to give us a portrait of the way we lived then (and now, for that matter), that was at once accurate and rather touching, went down the tubes—taking several years out of a promising directorial career as well, since Lester was not much heard from for almost seven years, until he came back with his swashbuckling spoof, **The Three Musketeers.** The hiatus was saddening, coming as it did when he was just getting good, and this movie proved that there was something more than modish flash in the manner he employed. To be both stylish and truthful was something that did not happen often in films of the sixties.

Rosemary's Baby

1968

Pray for the critic who must confront **Rosemary's Baby.** There must be some reasonable explanation for the popularity of Ira Levin's novel and the movie Roman Polanski based on it. But I am unable to say precisely what it is.

Rosemary's Baby, in both its incarnations, established beyond dispute that

Polanski takes a reading.

interest in the occult was something more than a cult phenomenon, that there was a mass audience for it, even though the success of **Baby** was not duplicated until it was surpassed in 1974 by **The Exorcist.** Even so, profitable imitators abounded on the paperback racks, at the movies, and on television during the intervening years, turning what had been an oddity into a genre, something that quickly established itself as a commonplace, quite unremarkable presence on the media scene during the late sixties and early seventies.

We can speculate that in an age when the irrational has itself become commonplace, people seek an explanation for the prevalence of the perverse and the downright evil in supernatural forces; how else explicate the inexplicable craziness of the times? In the particular instance of **Rosemary's Baby** we may also note an appeal to envy. In a generally prosperous epoch there are bound to be a very large number of people in much the same position as Rosemary's husband, the luckless actor played by John Cassavetes, people who imagine that the success of rather ordinarily talented people which they see all around them is the result of bargains with the devil, people who would be glad to strike a similar bargain should the opportunity present itself.

Finally, of course, we may note that the victims in both **Rosemary's Baby** and **The Exorcist** are children, one as yet unborn, the other almost an adolescent. In an age when the middle class tends to overprotect its children we are peculiarly horrified by their victimization. Or so we think. It may be that we are, in fact, guilty about the time and money we spend on them. Perhaps it gives us a perverse pleasure to see them abused in fictions of this kind. Certainly there is a strong sado-masochistic sexual current running beneath the surface —and not very far beneath it—in both pictures, which may or may not say something about the secret relationship a great many of us seem to have with our children, though it is often difficult to say who is the sadist, who the masochist.

But as I said, all of this is speculation. I don't share the general interest in the occult at all. It seems to me entirely witless, the energy expended on it completely misplaced. We have before us in our time too many unsolved problems that are subject to rational solution were we to put some effort—including that effort of understanding which worthwhile art represents—into them.

Which is not to say that I found **Rosemary's Baby** particularly deficient in craft. On the contrary, I thought Cassavetes, a man who has devoted a great deal of his career to directing films which are peculiarly sensitive to the needs and gifts of his actors, especially well-cast as the troubled thespian. So indeed, was Mia Farrow, whose only hope as an actress is to play an innocent and/or a victim. Roman Polanski, whose early absurdist works gave way to a middle period combined about equally of black humor, cynicism, and gothic horror—as Andrew Sarris remarks—was an excellent directorial choice. He created a suspension of disbelief that lasted as long as the picture was on—a considerable achievement considering how few colleagues managed it in derivative films.

For me, however, the rest is silence. I don't see what we, as a nation, see in this nonsense. I can't even see it as a relevant dreamwork which, if it were unravelled, would tell us something useful about the national psyche. Best call it an aberration and let it go at that.

The Lion in Winter

1968

The Lion in Winter was one of the worst messes of the decade. Mounted as if it were a "significant" historical pageant like **A Man for All Seasons** or **Becket,** acted as if it were Shakespeare, and written as if in imitation of Neil Simon, it was among the damnedest things I've ever seen.

One could imagine how James Goldman's little conceit—having important historical personages talk like the inhabi-tants of a television situation comedy—might, just might, have worked in a highly stylized the-atrical production. But the movies are a realistic medium. The stones of a movie castle are too, too solid. They rendered ludicrous Goldman's deliberate anachronisms. And Anthony Harvey's direction with its peculiar, misplaced emphasis on period detail—the actors crunching away on roast boar, flinging heavy metal goblets about, entering and departing sequences aboard horses or barges—only called attention to the dichotomy between author's intent and direc-tor's (and producer's) realization.

The story, if anyone cares, is about the squabble among the three sons of Henry II of England over who shall succeed him on the throne, with the old gentleman support-ing John; his estranged wife, Eleanor of Ac-quitaine, supporting Richard (latterly "the Lion-Hearted," but here a homosexual); and no one at all liking Geoffrey, who skulks and sulks a great deal. After almost two hours of piffle the issue remains essentially unresolved, essen-tially, indeed, where it was when the movie began. Henry was played heartily by Peter O'Toole, which was the correct strategy—brazen-ing it out, as it were. Eleanor, however, was played tremulously by Katharine Hepburn, in one of that rare actress's rare mistakes. She probably should not have attempted to play wife to an actor who is, in fact, almost a quarter cen-tury younger. Certainly she should have under-stood that this was not a role to be taken as seriously, or played as big, as she did.

One's temptation was to dis-creetly avert one's eyes, as one does from awful accidents. Unfortunately, however, other people kept pointing at it, telling us that far from being a disaster this was a great success. The New York Film Critics named **The Lion in Winter** the best picture of the year and the motion picture Academy presented Miss Hepburn with half of its prize for best actress (she tied with Barbra Streisand), her second consecutive Oscar and the third of her distinguished lifetime.

Now, **The Lion in Winter** was not appreciably worse than at least a dozen pompous, all-talking pictures which this group −traditionally wowed by fancy screenwriting −had presented with its palm. And one certainly begrudged Miss Hepburn nothing; it was easy to name a half-dozen wonderful performances by her which the prize-givers had missed.

But it was as Pauline Kael said in a cruelly accurate review of the film: "she draws upon our feelings for **her,** not for the character she's playing...it's self-exploitation, and it's horrible."

At any rate, it was saddening, for as Miss Kael pointed out, Hepburn's independence, her prickly pride in the way she had fought the studios in the old days, had previously done nothing to make her seem lovable in our eyes except to be uncompromisingly herself; and this had been the source of the respect, even awe, with which we had regarded her. And it was the basis, as well, for the natural affection that had flowed from the audience to her. To see her as she was in **Lion** indeed engendered the feeling "of dismay, and even of betrayal" of which Miss Kael wrote at the time.

Miss Hepburn, it would seem, weathered her crisis in confidence. In more recent performances and appearances she has been her old, spikey self, and one dislikes even bringing up what must be seen, in perspective, as a minor gaffe in an otherwise almost impeccable star career. It is perhaps a measure of

Kate Hepburn reflects on Director Anthony Harvey.

the American film industry's desperate desire to cling to the shreds of its former glory that it should single out this dubious bit of business for the dubious immortality of an Academy Award. One feels that, unconsciously, the actress's self-pity mirrored Hollywood's own self-pity, which had been growing steadily for a couple of decades and which was joggled anew each time one of its old, familiar faces (like Spencer Tracy, who died that year) passed from the scene, or as new film forms and styles attracted attention and took business away from the beloved, classic genres. (The runner-up in the New York Film Critics' voting that year was John Cassavetes' homemade, improvisational **Faces.**) Indeed, I think both critics and industry wilfully mistook **The Lion in Winter** for something it wasn't: either a fake-serious historical drama, or maybe even an old-fashioned Errol Flynn swashbuckler from which the action sequences were mysteriously mislaid, so that they could go on pretending for a little while longer that things had not changed. In the long run, perhaps, it doesn't make any difference. Junk is junk and it may be the idlest sort of idiot savantry to insist that this was a new, unprecedented sort of junk instead of the same old stuff. Still, the historical record ought to be made clear about such matters, even if it is only for the sake of tidiness.

They Shoot Horses, Don't They?

1969

Horace McCoy was that rarity of the politicized thirties, an instinctive existentialist and a sometime screenwriter who actually wrote serious fiction instead of merely talking about how he was going to someday. Thus, his cinematically constructed, tautly written little novels about the American lower depths–of which **They Shoot Horses** was the best known in an underground sort of way–were not much appreciated when they appeared. Those who were leftwardly tilted politically found his characters lacking in the romantic political consciousness they required in proletarian fiction. Nonpolitical readers suspected his Hollywood roots and his attraction to violent incident; he came perilously close on occasion to being a crime writer something like W. R. Burnett. McCoy was, in fact–and at his best–working something like the territory that interested Nathanael West. It may be that had he had better connections with the Eastern literary world, as West did, and had his career been dramatically snuffed out in an accident, as West's was, instead of sputtering out in drink and despair, he would have fared as well with posterity as West has.

Be that as it may, he would doubtless have been surprised at the movie version of **They Shoot Horses** which appeared late in 1969. Its creation was partly motivated, one imagines, by nostalgia. For it offered director Sidney Pollack an opportunity to colorfully re-create one of the more curious phenomena of an historical period in which there is now renewed interest–one of those marathon dances which attracted so much interest in the tabloid newspapers of the thirties and which seem to us such a pathetic and degrading experience for those desperate souls whom circumstances forced to enter (as well as for the spectators of their ghastly struggle against exhaustion) for prizes that were paltry. It is also clear, from the comments of the film's star, Jane Fonda, that those involved in the movie saw in it what had not been obvious to most readers when the book first appeared, namely that, whether it was intentional or not, it was possible to see in the marathon dance a political metaphor—insane effort devoted to the pursuit of an unworthy capitalist goal. This, I think, reduced McCoy's symbolism grievously. He was after bigger game than that rather limited bit of social criticism.

Still, that was certainly an element in his thinking and it is fair to note that despite the slickness and expansiveness of this production—rather at odds with the minimal art of the original novel—it was possible to pick up from it larger absurdist resonances. The meaningless chase after meaningless rewards is not confined to capitalist nations. A marathon dance will do as a metaphor for almost any kind of activity people devote themselves to with a zeal that exceeds common sense.

In the leading role, Jane Fonda, that capable and strong-minded woman, seemed miscast. It was difficult to believe she would reach such a level of despair that she would require her partner (played by Michael Sarrazin) to put her out of her misery, as if she were indeed a hopelessly wounded animal. Then, too, a flashback about the shooting of a beloved horse when he was a child failed to explain his willingness to do her bidding. Better to have left all that a mystery rather than offer so literal and feeble a motivation. Finally, the richness of the production went against the grain of the story. It was too carefully done; the reproduction of the old-time dance hall was so obviously perfect that it kept calling attention to its own cleverness.

On the other hand, there was

Director Sydney Pollack shooting horses.

a great deal to admire in the film. Susannah York and Red Buttons as the most prominent of the other contestants in the marathon were excellent, and Gig Young, as the cynical promoter of the marathon–a role suggested by only a few lines in the book–was simply superb. Never has the false cheer of the con artist been more perfectly rendered on the screen. In the end, indeed, the film triumphed over all its imperfections and the resistance to the work as a whole which they generated. Like it or not, one was affected by it. It is one of the few translations of a small novel into a large film which worked, one of the few in which the inflationary pressures of this movie age finally seemed unimportant in rendering a judgment on the work at hand. One was sorry that they were again present here, but glad that they did not undercut the effect of the film.

Catch-22
1970

Catch-22 was the ultimate expression, on film, of the sixties' attitude, perhaps immortally summarized by Tom Wolfe as "radical chic," by which he meant the espousal of extremely leftist critiques of American society by the sophisticated and the celebrated, who, he implied, took this stance not out of any deep conviction but because it became the smart thing to do–like dining in certain restaurants or wearing the clothes of certain designers.

When it was published in 1960, Joseph Heller's absurdist novel found a ready audience among such taste makers. But it did not–and they did not at the time–fit Wolfe's

description. One would certainly not have described the novel as "prowar." But neither was its comedy primarily intended as "antiwar." Rather, it concentrated on the American air force during World War II as a paradigmatic big organization, anti-individualistic, bureaucratized, dehumanizing, a model in his view for the swollen corporations which, after the war, claimed so many souls and so much concerned attention from the social commentators. With its broad characterizations and wildly farcical situations, it addressed the condition of the org man in an extraordinarily appealing way and its success story was a unique one. The work engendered a highly emotional response from its publishers, and they went forth to promote it with a passion that merely mercenary motives could not have inspired. This sense of commitment communicated itself all down the line–to salesmen, reviewers, the public. As a result, the book not only sold well but it also became a lively center of literary and cultural debate for a much longer time than most best sellers do. In time, as the political mood among young people changed from passive to active, the book became one of the touchstones of what came to be known as "the counterculture," alias "the film generation." The logic of turning the book into a movie now became irresistible, especially since Mike Nichols, who had fashioned that other generational cult object, **The Graduate,** allowed himself to be persuaded to do the project.

The film, however, was not the book. Where the latter's tone was lightly mocking, the movie's was sullenly angry. And so it went throughout this re-rendering of Heller's tale. His characters were essentially good-natured cartoons, the film's ugly grotesques. Where his inventions had a breezy, slapdash, improvisational quality about them, the movie's

Star, technician, director.

seemed pretentious, overwrought, and excessively calculated. Where his work came out of an American tradition of comic literature, the film, while eclectic to a maddening degree, elaborately, expensively and ludicrously aped the European art-film tradition.

Heavy of hand and slow of foot—but those were not the fundamental problems with **Catch-22.** Rather they were the consequences of its central flaw, which was the determination to more intensely politicize it. Both Nichols and his screenwriter, Buck Henry, seemed determined to find every conceivable opportunity to prove how much they hated war, to make a statement in opposition to Vietnam. Thus, one incident from the book—the death of a replacement gunner shot on his first mission with the bombardier-hero, Yossarian—instead of being just one of many events which cause the

latter to desert, becomes the central one. The movie returns to it no less than three times. It "explains" Yossarian conveniently—the way Rosebud "explains" **Citizen Kane,** which is to say that it painfully oversimplifies the man. More important, though, this death is peculiarly gory and permits the director to slam away at his message about the waste and horror of war. What a good boy he is! What bad boys are the establishment for getting us into situations where such events are inevitable.

But what a wretched excuse for art this movie is. For the whole point of Heller's novel was to demonstrate precisely the opposite point. What makes us mad, finally, is not a single traumatic incident, but rather a lifetime's accretion of absurdities, irrationalities, petty stupidities, and sadisms. Moreover, he does not for a moment suggest that it is only Americans of the mid-twentieth century upon whom this condition is visited. His air force might have been any air force, the war it was engaged in any war. But it was one of the presumptions of radical-chic social criticism that the United States was somehow uniquely cursed, that the rest of the world lived in innocence from which we alone had fallen.

It was a stupid notion, born of an hysteria that claimed more victims among the cultural and intellectual elite than one would have imagined possible as late as 1963 or 1964. It is, further, a sign of how shallow their emotions were, how easily manipulated, that this mood has passed off as quickly as it arrived, leaving behind such monumental wrecks as this movie: a hideously expensive empty shell, containing scarcely a kernel of the truths contained in its source, and, so far as one can tell, a device that contributed nothing to its cause—the shortening of a tragic war.

There is a lesson in this that is almost too obvious to be pointed out, but perhaps should be, anyway, just for the record. The place where art and politics meet has been called by Lionel Trilling a "bloody crossroads." It is, as films like this prove, a place to be avoided at all costs. The long road around it is the only one from which one can obtain the long view, those great visions which must be the basis for any worthwhile work of art.

Klute

1970

One of the marked characteristics of movie history in the sixties and, so far, into the seventies, has been the dwindling number of good roles for women and, consequently, a steadily diminishing number of women who are authentic movie stars; performers, that is, whose presence in a film will add appreciably to its box-office income no matter what its quality. As this is written Barbra Streisand is probably the only actress who is also in this bottom-line sense a star.

There were, of course, a number of showy roles for women during the last decade and a half, but, as the critic Molly Haskell observes, they were mostly as "whores, quasi-whores, jilted mistresses, emotional cripples, drunks, daffy ingenues, Lolitas, kooks, sex-starved spinsters, psychotics, icebergs, zombies, and ballbreakers." Her listing, as any movie critic can testify, is an accurate one and you don't have to be a militant feminist to see that there is something terribly wrong with the world view of an industry that offers a range of roles at once so limited and so exotic to ac-

tresses. Nor does it require much acumen to understand why so few women have emerged as new stars in this period. How can you build up a following when these unappealing roles are all that are offered—and then only on an intermittent basis? In the old days men and women alike played in three and four pictures a year as the studios built them up, gave them steady exposure in pleasing roles, allowing them, quite naturally—if hard work is still deemed a natural thing—to build an audience for themselves.

In short, it has not been easy for a young woman to favorably impose herself on the audience's awareness in this period. Jane Fonda, to her great credit, did so, mostly by playing characters all over the dismal range Miss Haskell outlined, before deliberately slowing her career in part, one imagines, because she saw quite clearly the limits the times were imposing on her, in part because she wanted to devote more energy to the political causes that increasingly preoccupied her. Nevertheless, her last major performance in Alan J. Pakula's **Klute,** for which she won the Academy Award, in a way both summarized and transcended the tendencies of this historical moment. Bree Daniel was, to borrow some of Miss Haskell's terms, whore, kook, and emotional cripple with elements of the daffy and the iceberg thrown in as well.

All of which may simply be a way of saying that she was a character of considerable and intriguing depth. **Klute**'s plot—in which the title character (Donald Sutherland) is a small-town cop come to the big city to investigate the disappearance of his best friend, and Bree is the call girl who may or may not know something about it—is the least interesting element in the film. Indeed, this mystery is unravelled (for viewers, but not for the main characters) rather casually about halfway

through the film. What is interesting, indeed memorable, about the film is the delicate exfoliation of Bree's character as she tentatively enters into a relationship with Klute, who is a version of the classic American screen hero–strong, taciturn, omnicompetent, the very sort of man whom the girl (near hysterical with fear as the result of a series of menacing phone calls from a psychopath who has already murdered a couple of other call girls) has never had the occasion to meet in her line of work.

He is, of course, something of a fantasy construction. On the other hand, it is doubtful if anything less than a fantasy could interest Bree Daniels. She is not a hooker with a heart of gold. Or a heart of lead, either. Rather she is a woman who has not by any means accepted her lot. She is scrambling for a toehold as a model or actress, trying to fight her way out of the demimonde through ambition and psycho-

analysis. And as the film develops we see that she is a woman who cannot allow herself to be dominated by men, much less give herself to them. Her defense is her expertise as a sexual actress. Since she is skilled in determining the fantasies of her scared johns and encouraging them to act them out, she is able to dominate the sexual encounter and, therefore, her clients, without their even knowing it. She does not allow them to gain control over her by giving her pleasure. That she merely fakes because it is good for business.

All along, the tough image she presents to the world is balanced by glimpses of her essential loneliness and an almost unacknowledged hunger for something like a normal life. Thus the importance of the policeman, Klute, in her life. Accompanying him on his investigative rounds she begins to see her world through his highly moral eyes, begins to see that it is uglier than she had dared admit to herself. In effect, he shows her what her end will be if she does not finally learn to give herself to someone, freely and completely, without thought of self-protection.

Her progress toward a solution of the mystery of herself parallels his progress in the solution of the criminal mystery he is investigating, and the simultaneous solution of both "cases" makes for a peculiarly satisfying film. Miss Fonda's performance—mercurial, subtly-shaded, multilevelled—was, indeed, one of the decade's best. She was given the time to build a very complex character and she had the gift to do so brilliantly. Moreover, it should have satisfied her to do so. She does indeed "liberate" herself from imprisonment within the bonds of banal male fantasies and from the self-censorship these fancies impose on so many women. On the other hand—and healthily—her paradigmatic case is solved with the gentle help of a decent man, implying, as so much women's lib rhetoric does not, that such men may exist (or are at least worth imagining) and that they are valuable to women, even though they may be all too rare.

Anyway, this movie may be a first in that it indulges none of the male notions about prostitution, but shows us this archetypal creature largely from the feminine point of view. For that alone—and it is not the most important of the movie's virtues—it would deserve an affectionate place in memory. More significant, I think, is that it used the much-advocated, and then much debated, new sexual freedom of the screen directly as a means of exploring psychology, indirectly as an aid in explicating a significant social issue, women's liberation. There were very few commercial films in this era about which such a claim could be seriously advanced.

The Cowboys
1971

The great, or at least the most discussed westerns of the 1950s (the two terms are not necessarily synonymous), were self-consciously classical in form: **Shane, High Noon,** and better than either of them, but overlooked by middlebrow critics, Howard Hawks' **Rio Bravo.** These films presented the basic elements of the western myth sparsely, even starkly, emphasizing archetypes at the expense of novelty and narrative richness. What seemed at the time something of a renaissance for the form—or maybe a return to first principles—was actually a first confession of exhaustion.

This became perhaps more obvious in the sixties, when the western took yet another turn. The dominant director was Sam Peckinpah and almost all his work in this form—**Ride the High Country, The Wild Bunch, The Ballad of Cable Hogue, Junior Bonner**—either elegiacally or violently took as its theme the closing of the frontier. And whether major or minor, whether **Butch Cassidy and the Sundance Kid** or **Villa Rides,** almost all westerns by other hands in recent years have dealt with the impossibility of maintaining the wild, free ways of the Old West and, apparently more distressing to their makers, the impossibility of creating and maintaining strong male comradeship, the bonds of which can only be annealed by group adventuring in open country. It is odd that film makers have discovered this sense of loss only recently. After all, the historical West closed at just about the time people began to make western movies—movies of any kind, for that matter. Why it was as late as in the sixties that people started to make movies about it is something of a mystery. Or perhaps it is not. Perhaps psychologically the frontier remained open for Americans until that time; perhaps they felt vaguely that there were wild countries still left to them beyond the Pacific rim if they cared to seek them out, until the Vietnam adventure turned so sour on them.

Mostly these developments escaped the attention of the last great movie westerner, John Wayne. To be sure, he ceased playing romantically inclined leads in his westerns of the sixties, tending to take more patriarchal roles, the glorious climax of which was his Academy Award-winning portrayal of the battered, one-eyed, and comically disreputable Rooster Cogburn in 1969's **True Grit.** One suspected, however, that no deep, brooding thoughts about the declining potency of the old western myths went into Wayne's management of his career. Rather, one imagines, he was accommodating himself to importunate age with intelligence and a certain humorous grace.

The Cowboys, immediate successor to **True Grit,** however, made one wonder. In a way it was a parody of Wayne's greatest film, Hawks' **Red River.** Once again, he was a hard-up rancher who needed to get his herd to market in a hurry in order to stay solvent. This time, however, he was forced to recruit children as trail hands, and the brutalities visited upon them on the drive were vividly and disturbingly realized by the director, Mark Rydell. Worse, in the end Wayne himself was killed in a gunfight with bandits. One could not remember when the actor whose stock-in-trade was indestructability had been so used in a film. Combined with the employment of children in the story, which seemed to say that the frontier mythology exercises a hold only on the imma-

ture, the death of this last classically defined western hero seemed to close off the possibility of reviving the old verities of this form.

The picture, as a result, was that rarity, a Duke Wayne film that performed badly at the box office. His old fans, of course, were disappointed to see him embracing the new anti-western mode, while the younger audience apparently could not believe that a star so closely identified with the classic style would or could do so, and thus stayed away.

Perhaps nowhere was the disarray of the new Hollywood more clearly reflected than in the traumatic changes inflicted on the western during the last decade or so. It had been the movies' bread-and-butter genre. Not so long ago it was an industry truism that no one ever lost money on a western, so firmly did the form grip the popular imagination. Now the connection between this historical fantasy and the modern individual's fantasies about himself was severed. Indeed, most Americans no longer thought of themselves as lonely defenders of the right and the virtuous. They were members of corporate teams and moral questions were no longer unambiguously presented or simple to solve. It is true that an attempt was made to relocate the classic western hero—strong, quiet, self-reliant—on urban police forces. It is also true that some of these pictures—notably Clint Eastwood's **Dirty Harry,** and its successor, **Magnum Force**—were commercial winners (Wayne himself made an imitation, **McQ,** which fared feebly). But like the rip-off spaghetti westerns so profitably made in Italy in the sixties, they were curiously lacking in resonance, meaninglessly violent or violently meaningless—it's difficult to determine which.

Moreover, the directors who had had living links with the Old West, who had

Wil Andersen and his cowboys.

at least glimpsed its sunset days as youths (there was still something of a frontier atmosphere in California when the first picture makers arrived there just after the turn of the century) were dying and retiring. The people now making westerns knew about it not from life, but from the movies of their childhood. In short, neither the audience nor the people who made films could sustain their old, intense level of interest in the form, and one had the feeling, as the new westerns unrolled, that all concerned were more interested in mourning the lost innocence which had permitted the suspension of disbelief on which the western's popularity had been based

as much as they were the lost values it had endorsed. It was part of the general turn inward of the movies in these years, a general loss of contact with the objective world.

Anyway, Bob Willougby's highly stylized photographic record of **The Cowboys** turns out to be more historically evocative and more emotionally powerful than the film itself. And that, too, says something about the condition of the movies, the loosening of their grip on us as a mass, as a new decade opened. It is a condition, alas, that has not improved in the few years since. And is unlikely to improve in the years ahead.

Production Credits

From Here to Eternity

1953; 118 minutes
released by Columbia

Directed by	Fred Zinnemann
Produced by	Buddy Adler
Screenplay by	Daniel Taradash,
	adapted from the novel by
	James Jones
Photographed by	Burnett Guffey
Edited by	William Lyon
Art Direction by	Cary Odell
Music by	Morris Stoloff
Cast:	Burt Lancaster; Montgomery Clift;
	Deborah Kerr; Frank Sinatra;
	Donna Reed; Ernest Borgnine.

A Star Is Born

1954; 155 minutes
released by Warner Brothers

Directed by	George Cukor
Produced by	Sidney Luft
Screenplay by	Moss Hart
Photographed by	Sam Leavitt
Edited by	Folmar Blangsted
Art Direction by	Malcolm Bert
Musical Direction by	Ray Heindorf
Cast:	Judy Garland; James Mason;
	Jack Carson; Charles Bickford.

Rebel Without a Cause

1955; 111 minutes
released by Warner Brothers

Directed by	Nicholas Ray
Produced by	David Weisbart
Screenplay by	Stewart Stern, based on
	an Irving Shulman adaptation
	of a story by Nicholas Ray
Photographed by	Ernest Haller
Edited by	William Ziegler
Art Direction by	Malcolm Bert
Music by	Leonard Rosenman
Cast:	James Dean; Natalie Wood; Jim
	Backus; Ann Doran; Sal Mineo;
	William Hopper; Rochelle Hudson;
	Cory Allen; Dennis Hopper.

The Man With the Golden Arm

1956; 119 minutes
released by United Artists

Directed by	Otto Preminger
Produced by	Otto Preminger
Screenplay by	Walter Newman, Lewis Meltzer,
	and Otto Preminger, based on the
	novel by Nelson Algren
Photographed by	Sam Leavitt
Edited by	Louis R. Loeffler
Art Direction by	Joseph Wright
Music by	Elmer Bernstein
Cast:	Frank Sinatra; Eleanor Parker;
	Kim Novak; Arnold Stang;
	Darren McGavin.

The Caine Mutiny

1953; 125 minutes
released by Columbia

Directed by	Edward Dmytryk
Produced by	Stanley Kramer
Screenplay by	Stanley Roberts, based on
	the novel by Herman Wouk
Photographed by	Frank Planer
Edited by	William Lyon and Henry Batista
Art Direction by	Rudolph Sternad
Music by	Max Steiner
Cast:	Humphrey Bogart; Jose Ferrer;
	Van Johnson; Fred MacMurray.

Guys and Dolls

1955; 138 minutes
released by MGM

Directed by	Joseph L. Mankiewicz
Produced by	Samuel Goldwyn
Screenplay by	Joseph L. Mankiewicz
Photographed by	Harry Stradling
Edited by	Daniel Mandell
Art Direction by	Joseph Wright
Music by	Frank Loesser
Musical Direction by	Jay Blackton
Cast:	Marlon Brando; Jean Simmons;
	Frank Sinatra; Vivian Blaine;
	Robert Keith; Stubby Kaye;
	Sheldon Leonard; Regis Toomey.

Raintree County

1956; 187 minutes
released by MGM

Directed by	Edward Dmytryk
Produced by	David Lewis
Screenplay by	Millard Kaufman, based on
	the novel by Ross Lockridge, Jr.
Photographed by	Robert Surtees
Edited by	John Dunning
Art Direction by	Urie McCleary
Music by	Johnny Green
Cast:	Montgomery Clift; Elizabeth Taylor;
	Eva Marie Saint; Nigel Patrick;
	Lee Marvin; Rod Taylor; Agnes
	Moorehead; Walter Abel.

Ocean's 11

1960; 127 minutes
released by Warner Brothers

Directed by	Lewis Milestone
Produced by	Lewis Milestone
Screenplay by	Harry Brown and Charles Lederer, based on a story by Clayton Johnson and Jack Golden Russell
Photographed by	William Daniels
Edited by	Philip W. Anderson
Art Direction by	Nikolai Remisoff
Music by	Nelson Riddle
Cast:	Frank Sinatra; Dean Martin; Joey Bishop; Sammy Davis, Jr., Peter Lawford.

The Great Race

1965; 158 minutes
released by Warner Brothers

Directed by	Blake Edwards
Produced by	Martin Jurow
Screenplay by	Arthur Ross, based on a story by Blake Edwards and Arthur Ross
Photographed by	Russ Harlan
Edited by	Ralph Winters
Art Direction by	Ferdie Carrere
Music by	Henry Mancini
Cast:	Tony Curtis; Jack Lemmon; Natalie Wood; Peter Falk; Keenan Wynn; Larry Storch; Ross Martin; Marvin Kaplan; George Macready; Dorothy Provine; Vivian Vance; Arthur O'Connell.

Dr. Dolittle

1967; 152 minutes
released by 20th Century-Fox

Directed by	Richard Fleischer
Produced by	Arthur Jacobs
Screenplay by	Leslie Bricusse
Photographed by	Robert Surtees
Edited by	Marjorie Fowler
Art Direction by	Ed Graves
Music by	Leslie Bricusse
Cast:	Rex Harrison; Samantha Eggar; Anthony Newley; Peter Bull; William Dix; Richard Attenborough.

My Fair Lady

1963; 170 minutes
released by Warner Brothers

Directed by	George Cukor
Produced by	Jack L. Warner
Screenplay by	Alan J. Lerner
Photographed by	Harry Stradling
Edited by	William Ziegler
Art Direction by	Gene Allen
Music by	Frederick Loewe
Musical Direction by	André Previn
Cast:	Audrey Hepburn; Rex Harrison; Stanley Holloway; Wilfred Hyde-White; Gladys Cooper; Jeremy Brett.

Who's Afraid of Virginia Woolf?

1966; 129 minutes
released by Warner Brothers

Directed by	Mike Nichols
Produced by	Ernest Lehman
Screenplay by	Ernest Lehman, adapted from the play by Edward Albee
Photographed by	Haskell Wexler
Edited by	Sam O'Steen
Art Direction by	Richard Sylbert
Music by	Alex North
Cast:	Elizabeth Taylor; Richard Burton; Sandy Dennis; George Segal.

Marnie

1964; 130 minutes
released by Universal

Directed by	Alfred Hitchcock
Produced by	Alfred Hitchcock
Screenplay by	Jay Presson Allen, from the novel by Winston Graham
Photographed by	Robert Burks
Edited by	George Tomasini
Art Direction by	Robert Boyle
Music by	Bernard Hermann
Cast:	Tippi Hedren; Sean Connery; Diane Baker; Louise Latham; Martin Gabel; Alan Napier; Bob Sweeney.

A Man for All Seasons

1966; 120 minutes
released by Columbia

Directed by	Fred Zinnemann
Produced by	Fred Zinnemann
Screenplay by	Robert Bolt, based on his play
Photographed by	Ted Moore
Edited by	Ralph Kemplin
Art Direction by	John Box
Music by	Georges Delerue
Cast:	Paul Scofield; Wendy Hiller; Leo McKern; Robert Shaw; Orson Welles; Susannah York; Nigel Davenport; John Hurt; Corin Redgrave; Vanessa Redgrave.

The Graduate

1967; 105 minutes
released by Embassy

Directed by	Mike Nichols
Produced by	Lawrence Turman and Mike Nichols
Screenplay by	Buck Henry and Calder Willingham
Photographed by	Robert Surtees
Edited by	Sam O'Steen
Art Direction by	Richard Sylbert
Music by	Paul Simon
Musical Direction by	Dave Grusin
Cast:	Dustin Hoffman; Anne Bancroft; Katherine Ross; Murray Hamilton.

The Lion in Winter

1968; 134 minutes
released by Avco-Embassy

Directed by	Anthony Harvey
Produced by	Martin Poll
Screenplay by	James Goldman
Photographed by	Douglas Slocombe
Edited by	John Bloom
Art Direction by	Peter Murton
Music by	John Barry
Cast:	Peter O'Toole; Katharine Hepburn; Jane Merrow; John Castle; Timothy Dalton; Anthony Hopkins; Nigel Stock; Nigel Terry.

Klute

1970; 114 minutes
released by Warner Brothers

Directed by	Alan J. Pakula
Produced by	Alan J. Pakula and David Lange
Screenplay by	Andy and Dave Lewis
Photographed by	Gordon Willis
Edited by	Carl Lerner
Art Direction by	George Jenkins
Music by	Michael Small
Cast:	Jane Fonda; Donald Sutherland; Nathan George; Charles Cioffi; Roy Scheider.

Petulia

1968; 103 minutes
released by Warner Brothers-Seven Arts

Directed by	Richard Lester
Produced by	Raymond Wagner
Screenplay by	Lawrence B. Marcus, based on the novel by John Haase
Photographed by	Nicholas Roeg
Edited by	Antony Gibbs
Art Direction by	Tony Walton
Music by	John Barry
Cast:	Julie Christie; George C. Scott; Richard Chamberlain; Arthur Hill; Shirley Knight; Pippa Scott; Kathleen Widdoes; Joseph Cotten.

They Shoot Horses, Don't They?

1969; 129 minutes
released by Cinerama Releasing Corp.

Directed by	Sidney Pollack
Produced by	Irwin Winkler and Robert Chartoff
Screenplay by	James Pol and Robert E. Thompson, based on the novel by Horace McCoy
Photographed by	Philip Lathrop
Edited by	Frederic Steinkamp
Art Direction by	Harry Horner
Music by	Johnny Green
Cast:	Jane Fonda; Michael Sarrazin; Susannah York; Gig Young; Red Buttons; Bonnie Bedelia; Al Lewis.

The Cowboys

1971; 128 minutes
released by Warner Brothers

Directed by	Mark Rydell
Produced by	Mark Rydell
Screenplay by	Irving Ravetch, Harriet Frank, Jr., and William Dale Jennings
Photographed by	Robert Surtees
Edited by	Bob Swink and Neil Travis
Art Direction by	Philip Jefferies
Music by	John Williams
Cast:	John Wayne; Roscoe Lee Brown; A Martinez; Robert Carradine; Mike Pyeatt; Sean Kelly; Stephen Hudis; Al Barker, Jr.; Nicholas Beauvy; Sam O'Brien; Norman Howell; Clay O'Brien; Bruce Dern; Slim Pickens; Steve Benedict; Coleen Dewhurst; Sarah Cunningham; Matt Clark; Allyn McLerie.

Rosemary's Baby

1968; 134 minutes
released by Paramount

Directed by	Roman Polanski
Produced by	William Castle
Screenplay by	Roman Polanski, based on the novel by Ira Levin
Photographed by	William Fraker
Edited by	Sam O'Steen and Bob Wyman
Art Direction by	Richard Sylbert
Music by	Christopher Komeda
Cast:	Mia Farrow; John Cassavetes; Ruth Gordon; Sidney Blackmer; Maurice Evans; Ralph Bellamy; Angela Dorian; Patsy Kelly; Elisha Cook.

Catch-22

1970; 121 minutes
released by Paramount

Directed by	Mike Nichols
Produced by	John Calley and Martin Ransohoff
Screenplay by	Buck Henry, based on the novel by Joseph Heller
Photographed by	David Watkin
Edited by	Sam O'Steen
Art Direction by	Richard Sylbert
Music by	John Hammell
Cast:	Alan Arkin; Martin Balsam; Richard Benjamin; Bob Newhart; Art Garfunkel; Jack Gilford; Anthony Perkins; Paula Prentiss; Jon Voight; Orson Welles; Buck Henry; Martin Sheen; Bob Balaban.

From Here to Eternity

1953

Frank Sinatra gave Academy Award-winning performance as Corporal Maggio.

Sergeant Warden (Burt Lancaster)
defends Maggio against sadistic,
knife-wielding stockade guard,
Fatso Judson (above),
played by Ernest Borgnine
before he changed his
image with his Academy
Award-winning performance
in title role of Marty.

Robert E. Lee Prewitt (Montgomery Clift) and beloved bugle the system forbids him to play.

The Caine Mutiny

1953

Director Edward Dmytryk confers
with Van Johnson
about typhoon sequence in
which ``mutiny'' on U.S.S. Caine
actually takes place.

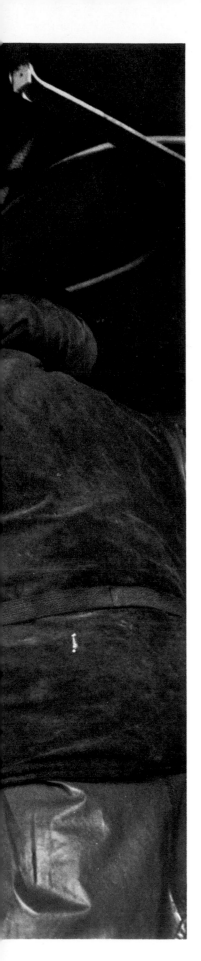

Height of storm, height of drama.
Lieutenant Maryk "takes the con" from Captain Queeg (Humphrey Bogart),
replacing him as ship's commanding officer on
grounds that he is no longer mentally fit to sail her.

A Star Is Born

1954

Director George Cukor and Judy Garland on set.
James Mason (r) played her husband, the fading, alcoholic
matinee idol, Norman Maine. Both were superb.
Following four pages:
A pensive Judy and three shots
from "Lose That Long Face," a number unfortunately
edited out of the film before release.

Rebel Without a Cause

1955

Guys and Dolls

1955

Brando's first dance rehearsal for
his role as Sky Masterson—
with choreographer Michael Kidd.
Willoughby:
"We went to the Sam Goldwyn rehearsal stage.
Frank Loesser was there to play
piano for us....Brando was in remarkable
physical condition. He was having
Kidd on, but all with great good nature.
This set is the only one
I've ever seen where Brando
looked as though he were enjoying himself."

The Man With the Golden Arm

1956

Preceding pages:

Frank Sinatra contemplates perhaps his most taxing role.

Preminger demonstrates to co-star Kim Novak how he wants a scene played.

Willoughby:

"It was a scene Kim just could not get.

I can't recall the actual number of takes, but it was astronomical.

In the cut film, Otto played it on Frank's face, with her voice over."

Above & right:

Famous withdrawal sequence in which Dealer quits heroin "cold turkey."

Preminger's mobile face is rarely in repose in camera's presence.

1956

Raintree County

Preceding pages:
Breeze is reserved for stars as locals watch slow process
of movie making in summer heat of Natchez, Mississippi.
Above & right:
Elizabeth Taylor's co-star was Montgomery Clift, trying to come back after
auto accident that scarred him physically and psychologically.
He required vitamin shots and oxygen to keep up pace on
a troubled and difficult production.
Observers on set recall Taylor's "almost motherly" concern for him.
Following pages:
Impressionistic study of Eva Marie Saint.
Marvelously cluttered set with ninety-eight people.

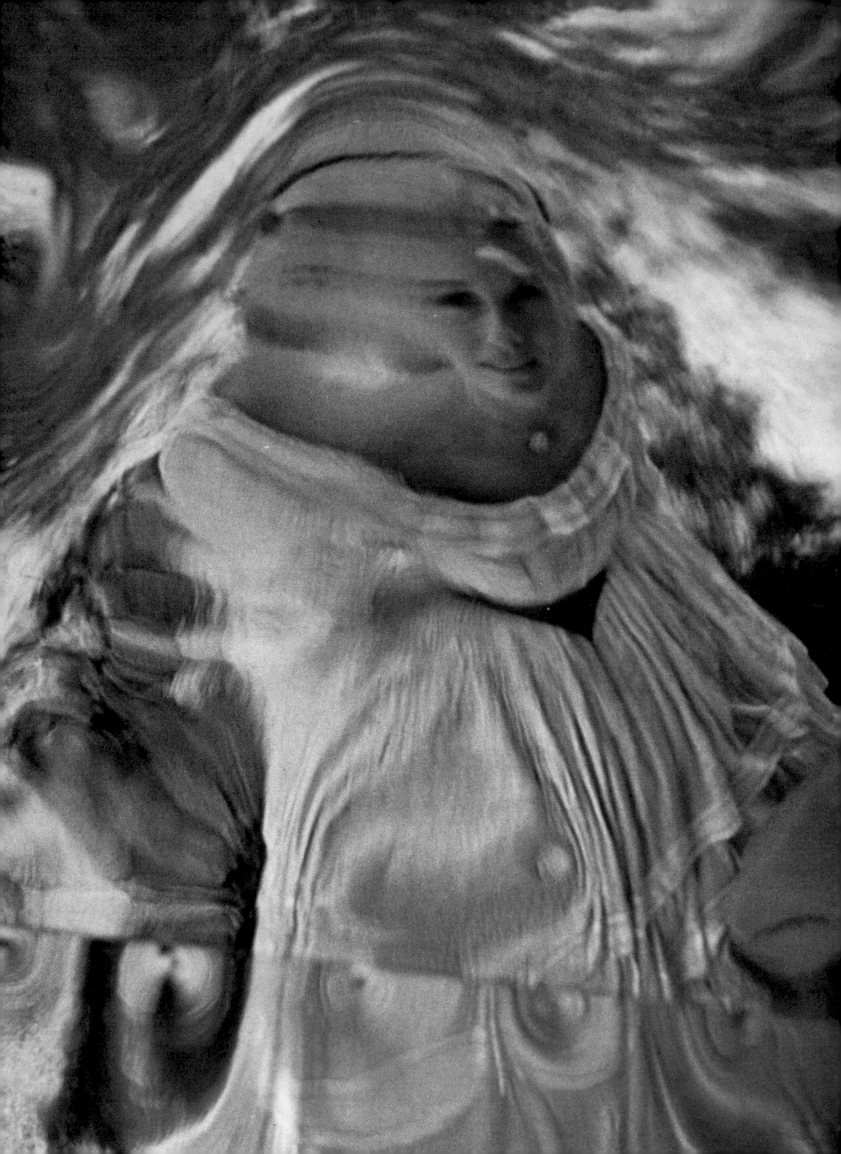

Lee Marvin with Clift.

Enemy rain halts shooting.
Ironically, given film's title, rain plagued production for weeks.
Right: Marvin as Flash Perkins, one of the character roles that led to stardom.
Following pages: Clift finds a moment of peace.

Ocean's 11

1960

Rat Pack cuts up on Las Vegas nightclub stage.

Life in Vegas.

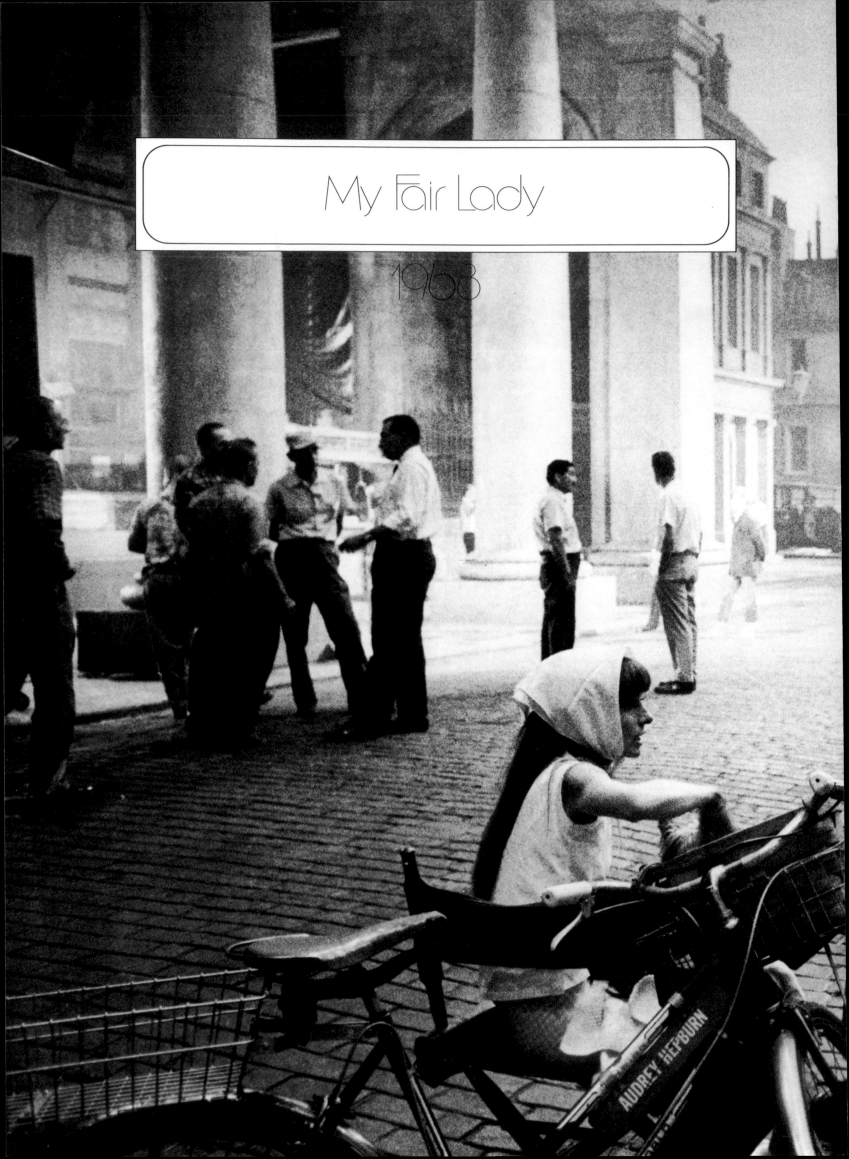

My Fair Lady

1958

London in Hollywood.
Preceding pages: Audrey Hepburn and George Cukor,
who won his only Academy Award for directing this film.
Below: Covent Garden.
Bottom & following pages: Rain stays mainly on Miss Hepburn.
Director Cukor's closed set made still photography difficult.

Rex Harrison
as Henry Higgins insists
on cleanup for
Eliza (below).
But no force on earth can
clean up her dustman
father, played
by Stanley Holloway (r).

Body Language: From Harrison to Cukor to Harrison.

The way it was.
Or the way we like to think it was.
A montage of Edwardian life as recreated
in beautiful downtown Burbank.

Marnie

1964

Preceding pages:
Hitchcock will go to any lengths to get a masterful traveling shot.
For this one, technicians had to construct a breakaway balcony.
These pages:
Ominous shadows are master director showing Sean Connery and
Tippi Hedren how to play a scene.
Following pages:
Connery, Diane Baker.

The Great Race

1965

Preceding pages:
Storm sequence in North Pacific Ocean
required an entire sound stage at Warner Brothers.
Left & below: Jack Lemmon.
Right: Natalie Wood.

Hero Tony Curtis always wore white.
Air shot of balloon ascension was taken by remote-control camera on helicopter.

Here & on following pages:
Special Effects Department triumphs again.
Willoughby:
"Only the long arm of the Chapman crane could reach across the
water to the actors on the `iceberg,'
and there was certainly no place for a still man to hop aboard.
But I was able to attach one of my remotes—a motor-driven Nikon
with radio receiver attached—to the movie camera.
(Aerial can be seen, opposite, extending up from
movie camera's matte box.)
I had two transmitters, each with five sending channels,
so I could set off three or
four cameras at once, or trigger them off one at a time.
During the storm sequence,
the waves were so fierce that I had to case all the cameras
in plastic bags, with just a little hole for the lens."

Willoughby:
"Picture of Tony Curtis diving was shot by remote attached to movie camera.
I also shot from the side of the set with a long lens.
The two cameras were hooked up, so that both shot simultaneously."

Great Custard-Pie Fight took five days to film.
According to Publicity,
it was the biggest pie fight ever.
No doubt.
"Less is more" was an aesthetic criterion rarely
observed during the Platinum Years.
Willoughby:
"With pies flying everywhere, there was
just no place to stand.
Again it proved practical to hide a couple of
remotes on the set —
with plastic covers, of course."

Director Blake Edwards aims pie at Natalie Wood.

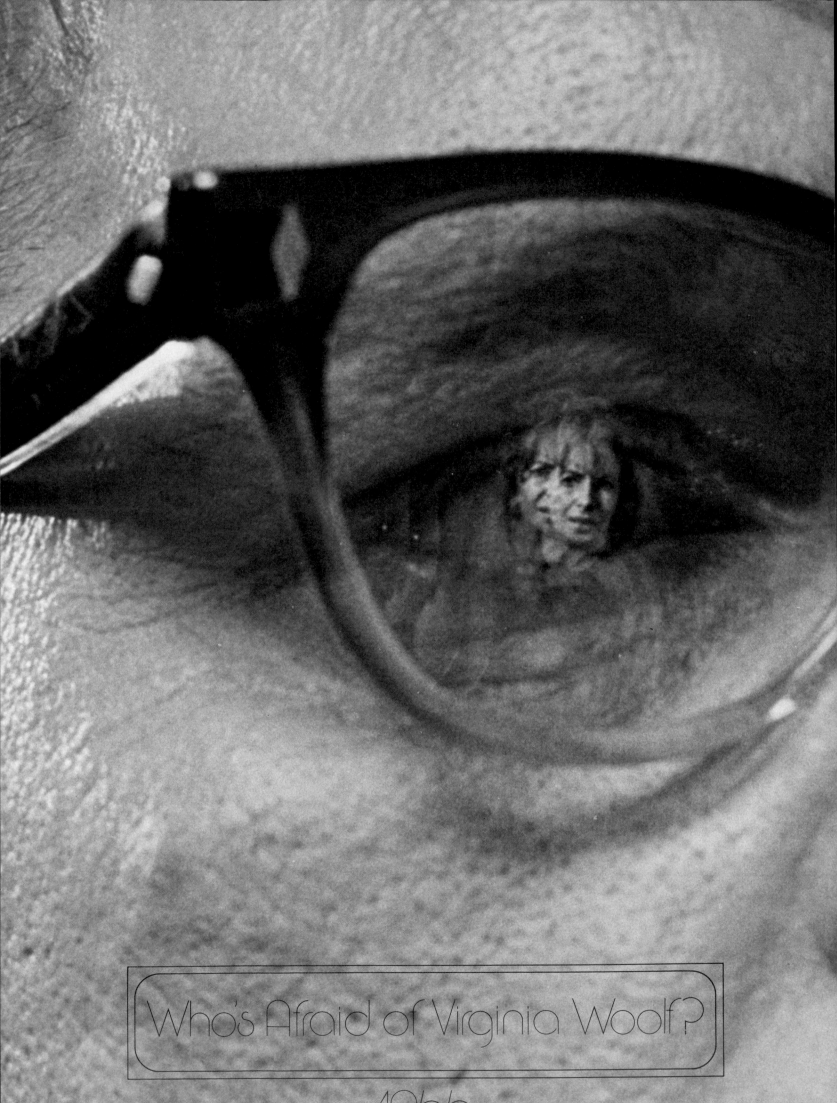

Who's Afraid of Virginia Woolf?

1966

"It was a very hard set to work on," Willoughby recalls.
"The actors were keyed up and there was nervous tension everywhere."
The Burtons and director Mike Nichols (with Taylor, opposite),
who was doing his first film, closeted themselves away to work on their
interpretations of Albee's play.
Willoughby:
"In drinking scenes I used an extreme wide-angle lens and forced
the distortion to give that alcoholic-haze feeling."

The basic triangle:
Young marrieds (George Segal and
Sandy Dennis, above) are briefly put asunder
by rapacious Martha, with violent results.
Film was in black and white,
and cinematographer Haskell Wexler, who
won an Oscar, kept the light level
so low that Willoughby had to acquire a
special lens to shoot candid color.

Opening up the play.
Nichols moved his actors outdoors for one key sequence.
And, of course, he could show the sexual encounter which in those
discreet days could only be alluded to on the stage.

Nichols and his stars in final scene.

A Man for All Seasons

1966

Preceding pages:
The Man for All Seasons
(Paul Scofield) and his sovereign (Robert Shaw).
Above, right, & following pages:
Sir Thomas's daughter, prettily played by Susannah York.
Willoughby's camera contrasts
Scofield's careworn countenance with her fresh beauty.

Dr. Harrison. Anthony Newley (r) and Samantha Eggar.

Dr. Dolittle

1967

Carnival featuring Pushmi-pullyu
was one of film's high points.
Willoughby:
"They shot it at little Castle Combe,
near Bath, the ideal English village.
But troubles plagued them from start to finish.
First, they had villagers who didn't
want them in. The weather was terrible.
And there were complications and
delays because of the animals.
If it hadn't been so damaging financially
to Fox, it would have been laughable."

The Graduate

1967

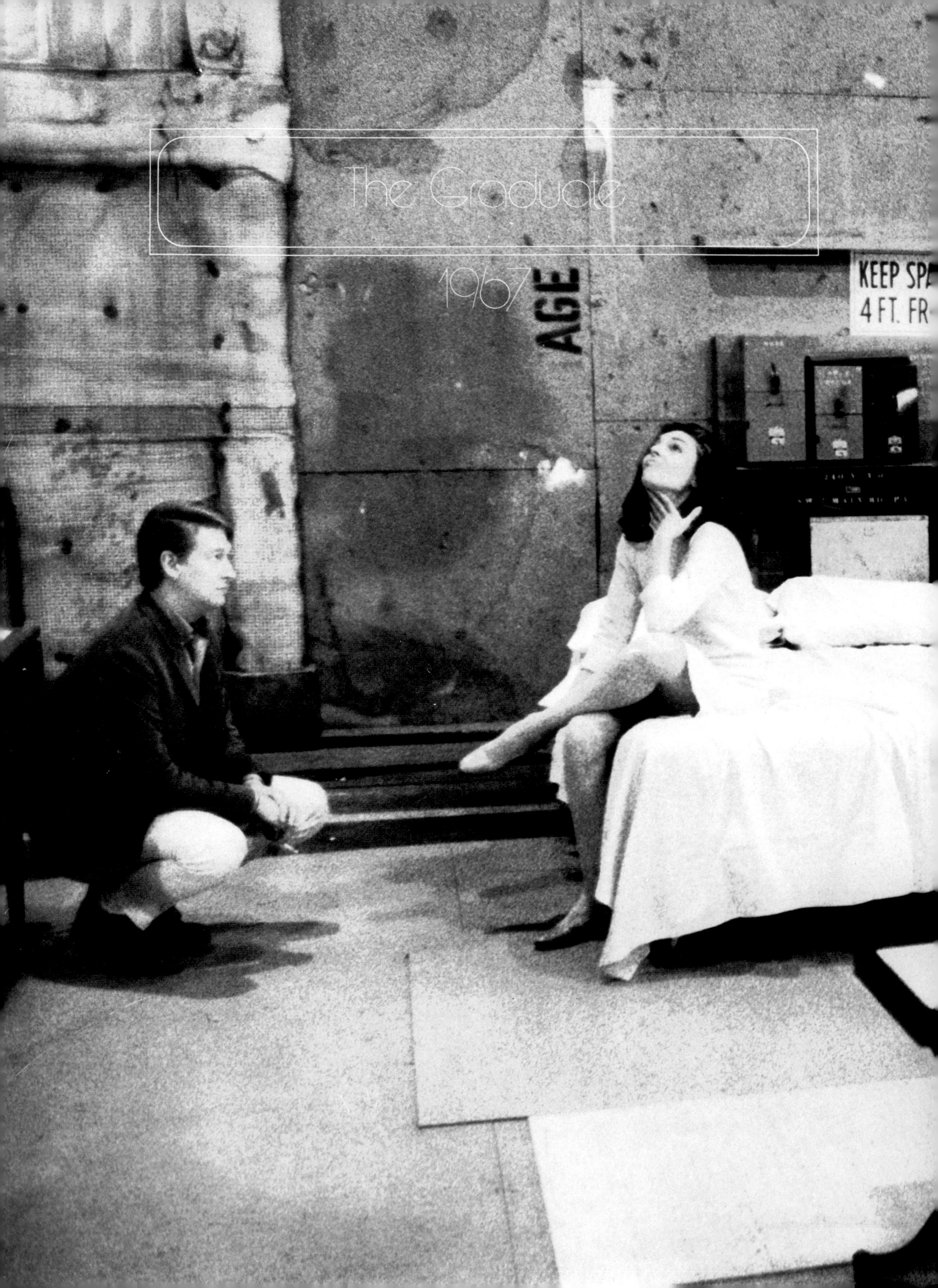

From Rehearsal to Reality:
Mike Nichols, Anne Bancroft, Dustin Hoffman.
Willoughby:
"This was the second film I did with Nichols.
It was shot at Paramount, and I vividly recall getting to the sound
stage as Nichols was putting a scene together.
It was really exciting to watch and the first time I ever saw one explode like this.
I guess Anne Bancroft and Dustin Hoffman came with ideas of
how the scene should play; it all looked good to me
— better than most of the things I had been working on, for certain.
Nichols watched with approval, smiling, as the actors went through their paces.
It was only after that he said, quite offhand, 'Why not play it for laughs?'
They tried it and it became better than good.
It was electric.
Well, I was a Nichols fan from then on — at least as a director."

Silhouetted: Katherine Ross (I) as Miss Robinson, and Hoffman.

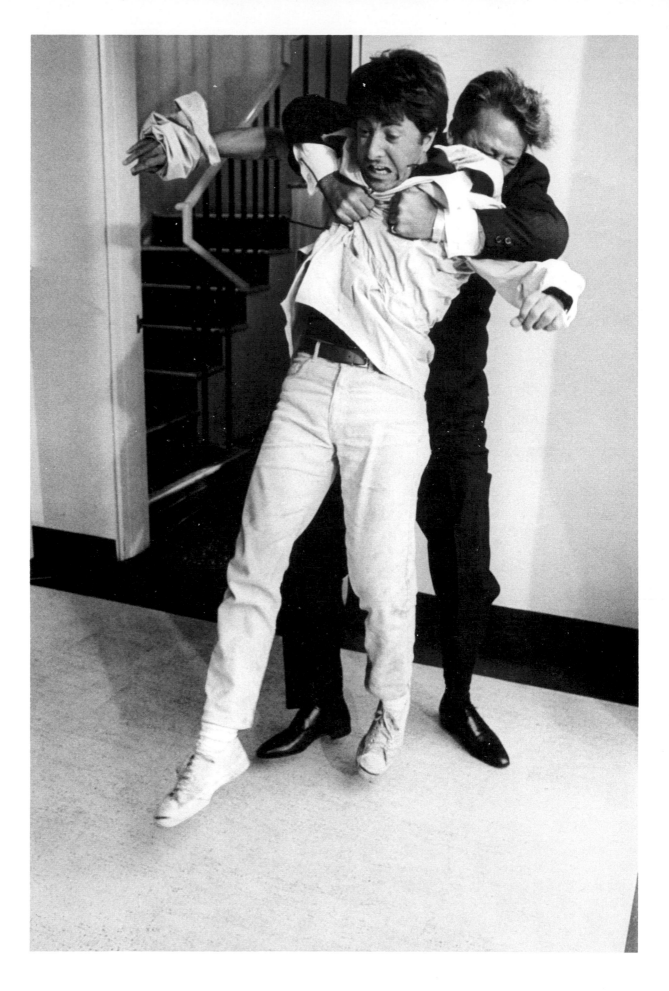

Mr. Robinson (Murray Hamilton) has his only inning.

Wedding Sequence:
Elaine is about to marry the wrong man.
But is The Graduate the right one?
Willoughby:
"Because of the nature of this film, everything I shot was candid.
It was frustrating not being able to get into those cramped little sets.
I got most pictures by poking my zoom lens through
scenery flats and open parts of sets....
One of the more successful series is the wedding sequence,
starting from the shot of him against the back window.
It moves very fast.
I probably used a 20mm lens for this, and you have no idea how
close that swinging cross was coming to me at times.
I was right in the crush of director, hand-held camera, script supervisor....
It was wild!"

Petulia

1968

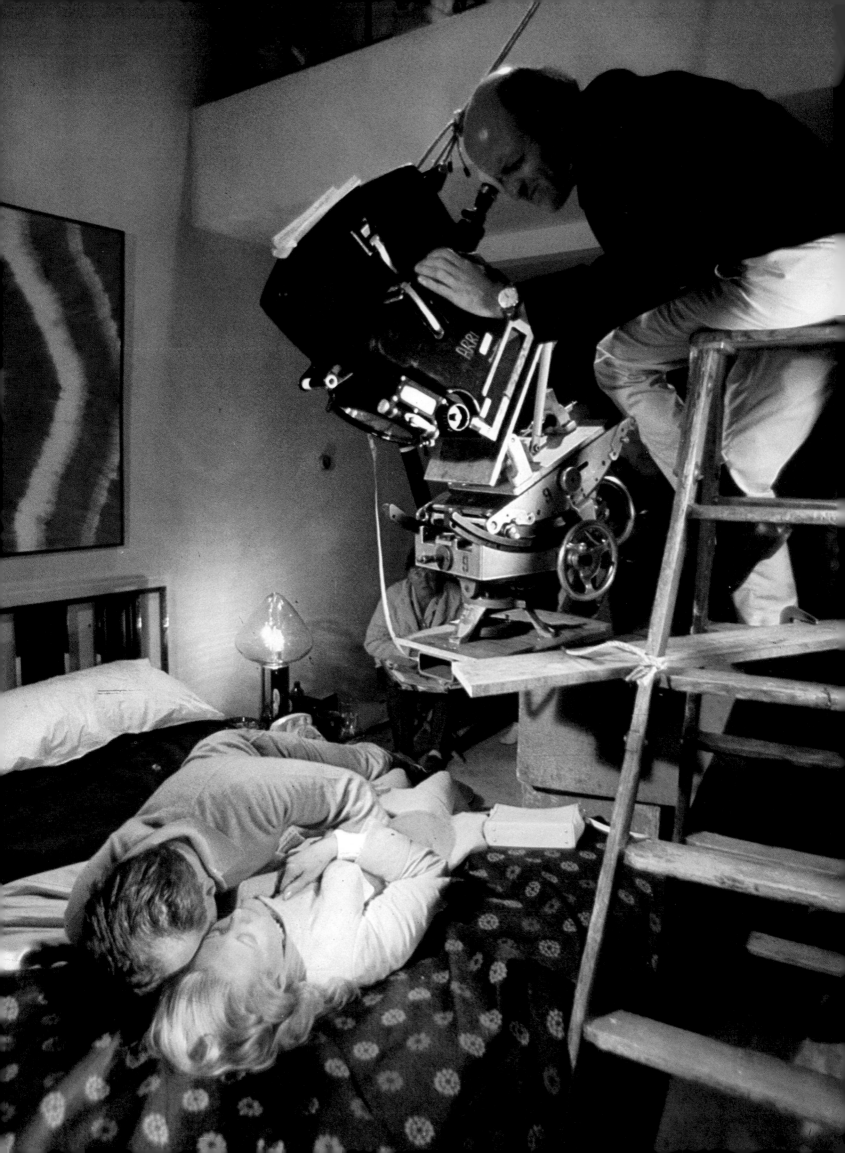

Preceding pages:
Director Richard Lester at work and at rest.
Tuba was something Petulia played to demonstrate
her kookiness.
George C. Scott was troubled older
man who tried to bring a sense of order into Petulia's life,
something he never offered his wife (Shirley Knight, above).
Richard Chamberlain (r) was Petulia's unhappy mate.

Petulia (Julie Christie).
Lester directs and, after a moment,
Scott gets the message.
Willoughby:
"I shot Petulia and The Graduate at the
same time, so there was a lot
of flying back and forth,
San Francisco to Los Angeles.
Petulia was one of the more unusual film
experiences I've had.
Dick Lester had a script,
which I read and thought I understood.
But after two days I had to pull
him aside and ask him what was happening.
Hardly anything I had read in the script
was being shot.
He was vague, but I gathered
he wanted an improvisational air.
Life is full of unrelated happenings,
he said, and nothing is ever
really concrete in the way it happens....
Dick also was shooting in
a different way.
On every take he had a
second camera, with a long zoom lens,
concentrating on the actors' hands, or
eyes, or whatever looked interesting.
When one actor asked George Scott
what had been photographed during
one scene, George said he was
damned if he knew....
I said to Dick when I left
that sometime I hoped to work on the
same film with him.
It was a strange movie,
although evidently it all worked out
pretty well in the end."

Rosemarys Baby

1968

Opening pages:
An average young American couple
(John Cassavetes and Mia Farrow) —
before giving the devil his due.
Following spread: Rosemary.
These pages: Making a movie.

Witching Hour:
Ruth Gordon and new
recruit Cassavetes
in dream orgy at which
devil invades Rosemary.
Miss Gordon won
an Academy Award for
her performance.

Ralph Bellamy (l)
and Sidney Blackmer,
in his last screen role,
as two members of the coven.
Below: Rosemary clutches sink,
momentarily overcome
after eating neighbor's mousse.
Steam — to suggest
hot water — was blown into picture
by director Roman Polanski
(''a dream to work with''),
who laughingly told Willoughby,
''You've got the most
expensive special-effects man in
Hollywood working for you.''

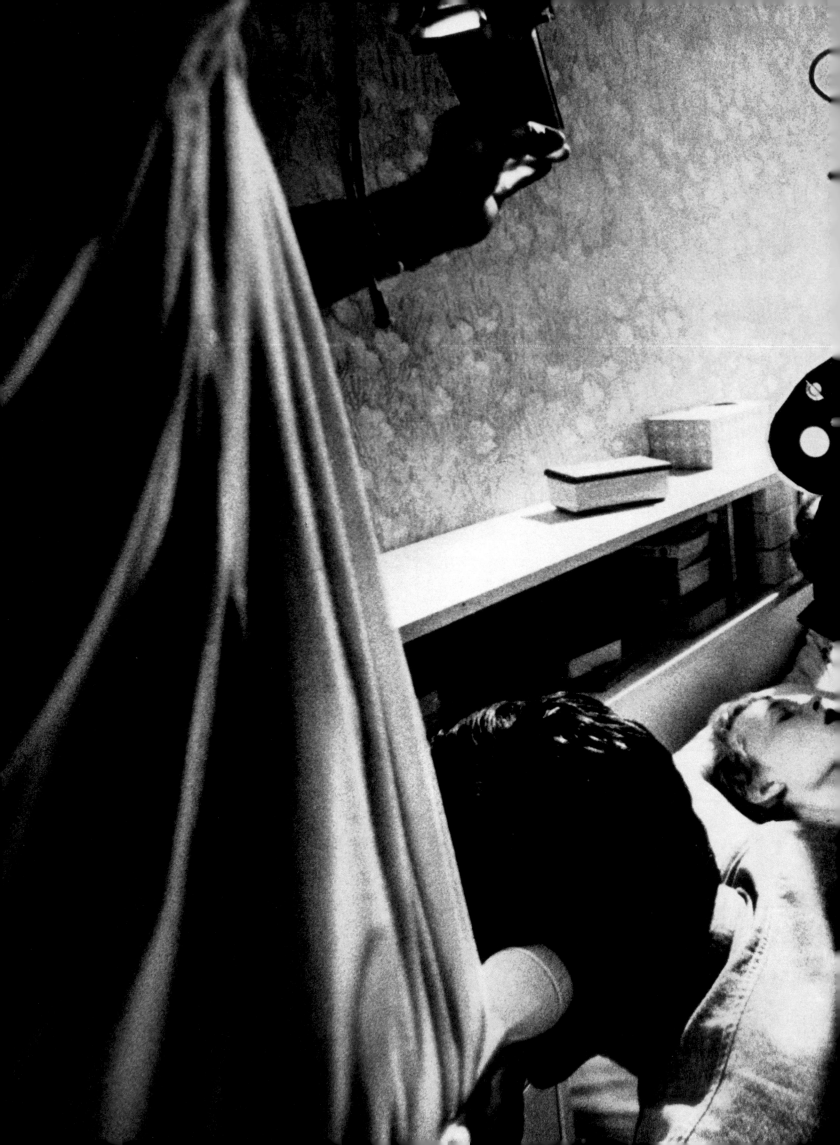

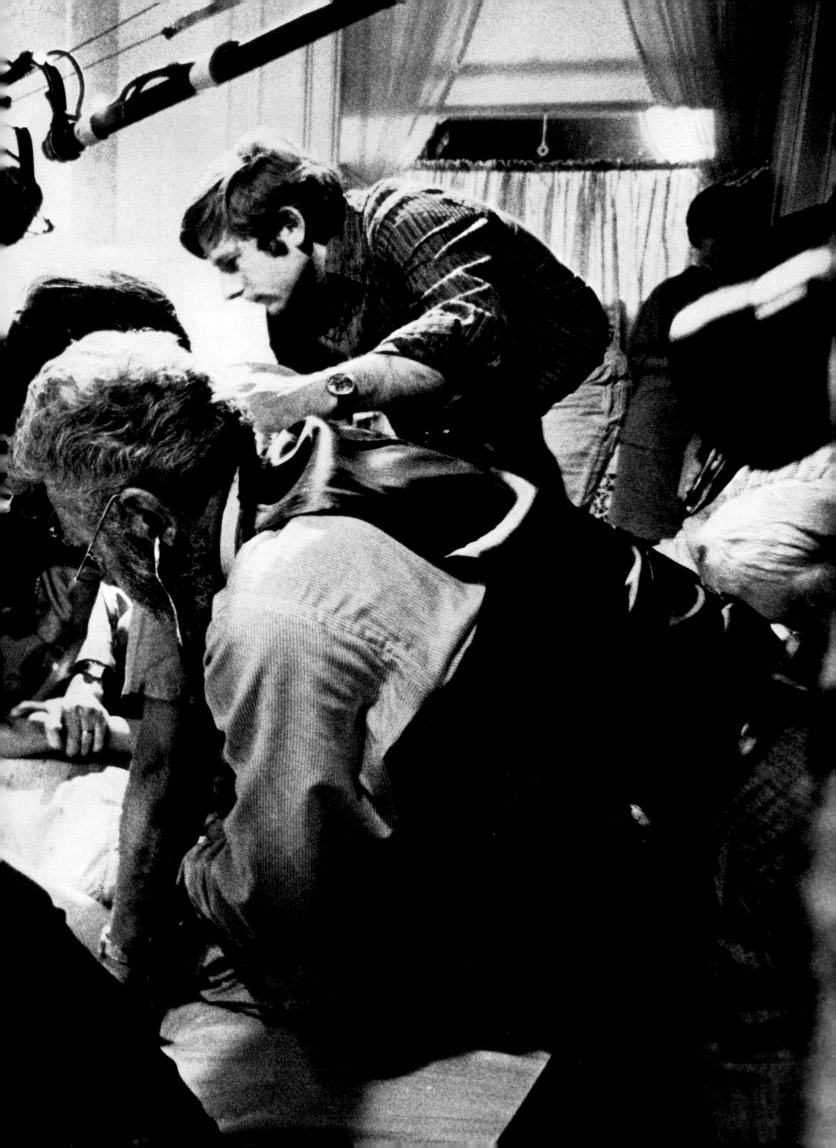

The Lion in Winter

1968

Katharine Hepburn as Eleanor of Aquitaine,
Peter O'Toole as Henry II of England.
Willoughby: "The combination is rather heroic and the force of energy is overwhelming."

Preceding pages:
A regal presence, no matter what the costume.
Below: A king's ire. Right: Ready to roll.
Willoughby:
"If the still photographer is low man on the totem pole in Hollywood,
he's even lower in England.
The crew is fantastic and very helpful, but
the assistant director rules the floor and stands
as buffer between the director and actors and any outside element,
and you just can't break this down.
Once, I was sitting in a corner disgruntled because I couldn't shoot a scene, and
Kate Hepburn stopped and asked why I wasn't up where the action was.
When I told her, she stopped the
rehearsal and told the director the scene should be photographed.
He was so nonplussed he said okay.
Kate showed me where to stand for the best shot, gave me a wink,
and retired to the back of the set.
A patron saint of still photographers.
How often on other foreign films I've wished she were around."

Princess Alais was played by Jane Merrow.
Opposite: A lioness and her favorite cub. Richard was played by Anthony Hopkins.

They Shoot Horses, Don't They?

1969

Preceding pages:
Doomed Gloria (Jane Fonda) and
Alice (Susannah York), who survived.
These pages: Fonda and Al Lewis, Bonnie Bedelia,
Fonda in women's dormitory.
Following pages: Master shot of marathon-dance hall.
Willoughby:
"With director Sydney Pollack I had the ideal relationship.
The crew also was super....
On the dance-hall set, Sydney was using a
360-degree shot most of the time
as the actors went round and round the track.
It soon became clear that from my one, high-angle location
I wasn't going to get many usable frames.
So Sydney and the crew let me clamp a
radio-controlled camera on the dolly carrying their
hand-held master camera, so I was always
pointed at the action as directly as they were.
I had a second camera hidden in the
bunting at the front of the grandstand and, again with
Sydney's approval, asked the actors
to make their play as they passed that point.
The resulting pictures of 'the Sprint'
speak for themselves, I think."

York and Michael Sarrazin.
Opposite: Gig Young won an Oscar for his performance as Rocky, the promoter.

The Sprint.

Beginning of the end for Sailor (Red Buttons), whose heart gives out.

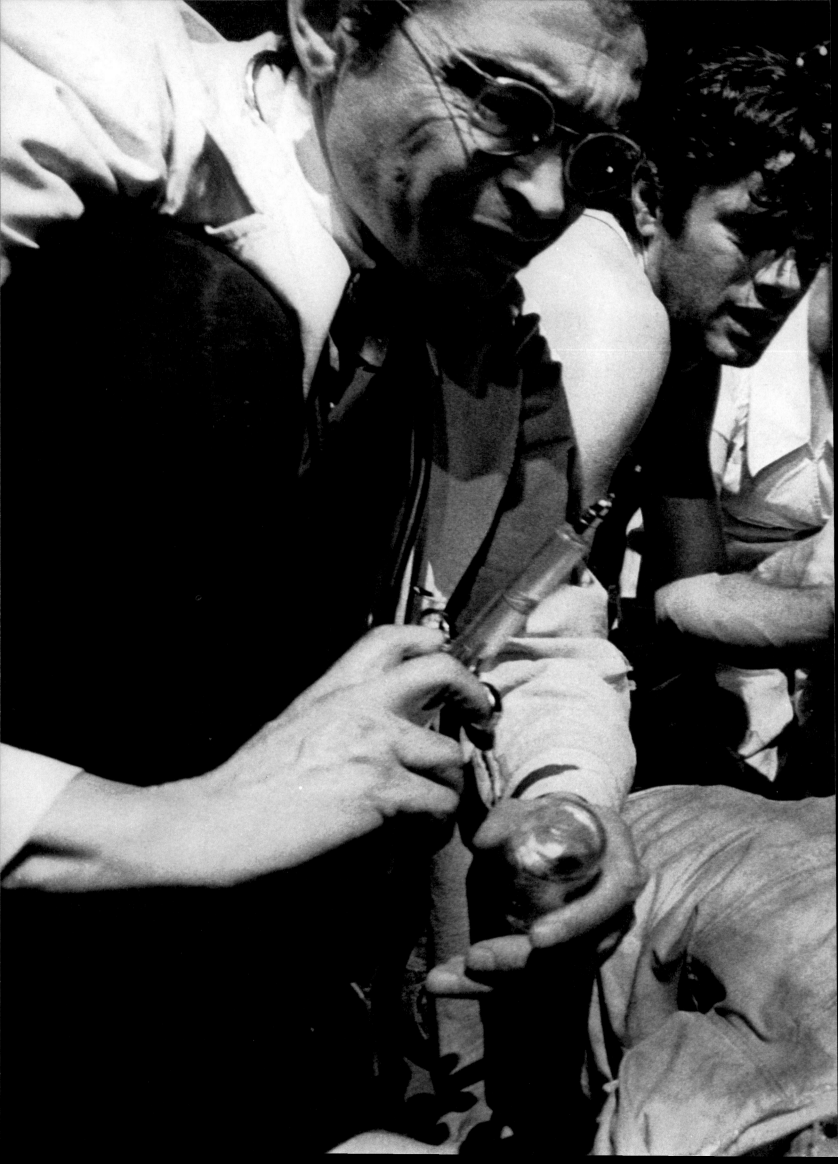

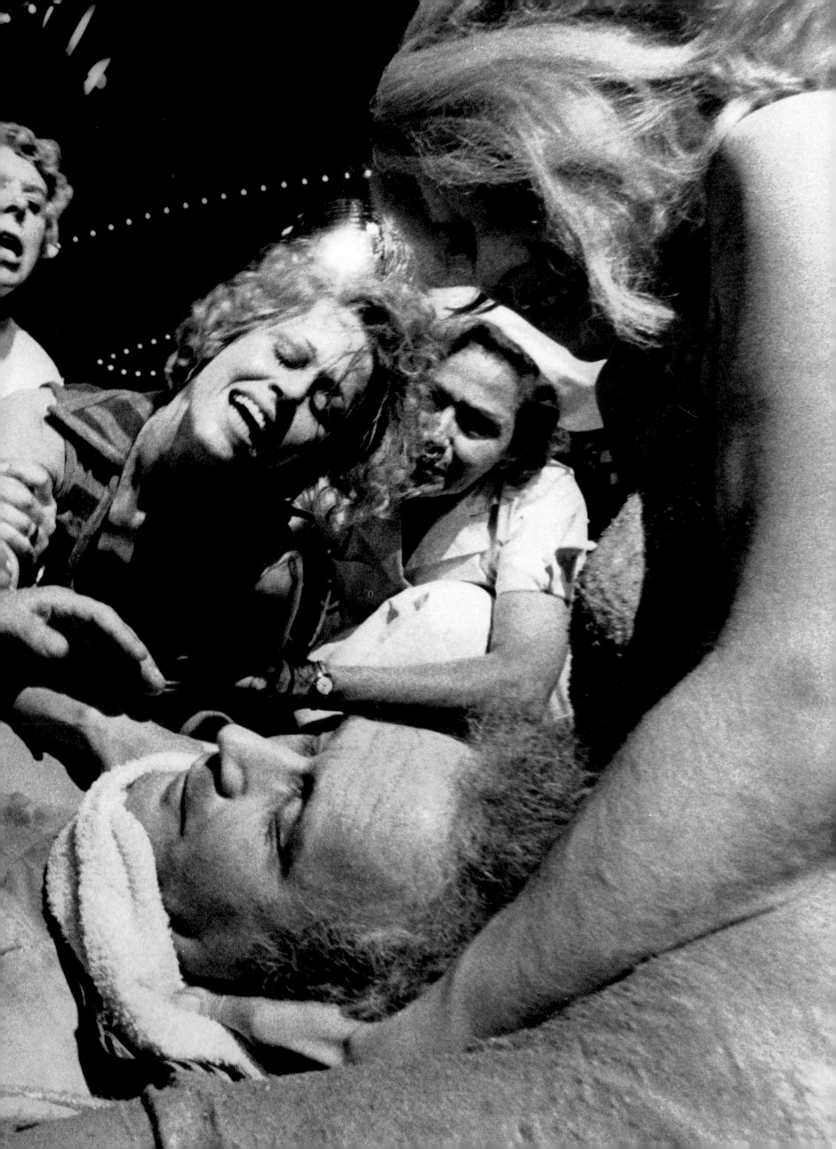

Yossarian (Alan Arkin) and Nurse Duckett (Paula Prentiss).

Catch-22

1970

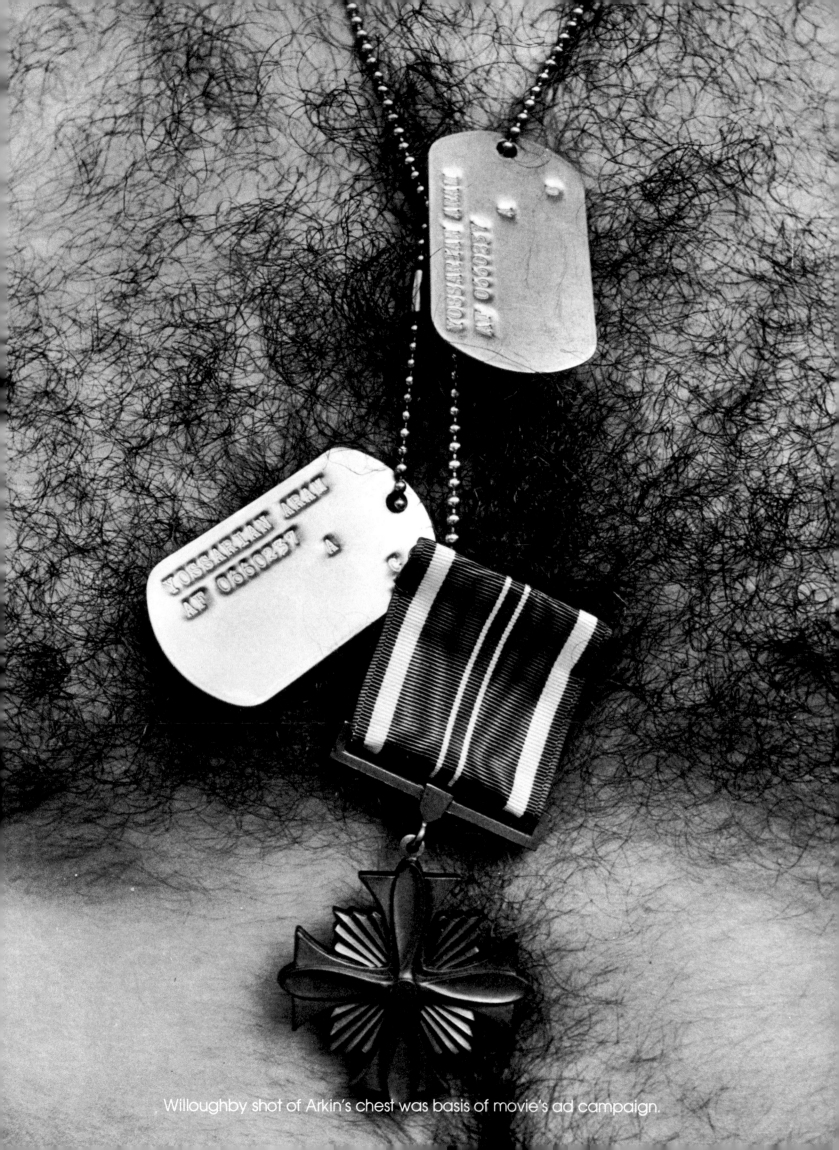

Willoughby shot of Arkin's chest was basis of movie's ad campaign.

Ancient B-25's take off, erratically.
Willoughby:
"Because these planes were designed for a big bomb load,
they got in trouble flying empty for the movie.
The minute one got in the prop wash of another, it would
waggle all over the field.
The cinematographer wanted a mass take-off for dramatic impact."

I set up my gear and stationed myself on a nearby rise.
As one group got off, I started
activating my 300mm and suddenly heard someone yell,
'Look out!' I spun around and here is a bleeding B-25,
struggling to get airborne, just over my head!
I hit the dust, spitting and swearing, but luckily I kept my
finger on the transmitter button and got my pictures."

Clockwise from left:
Major Major (Bob Newhart),
Milo Minderbinder (Jon Voight)
with Colonel Cathcart (Martin Balsam),
and Chaplain Tappmar
(Anthony Perkins).

Clockwise from top left:
Milo Minderbinder (Jon Voight),
Colonel Cathcart (Balsam), and Colonel Corn
(Buck Henry, who doubled as
screenwriter), General Dreedle (Orson Welles),
Captain Orr (Bob Balaban),
Major Danby (Richard Benjamin).

Brothel scene—a study in the Fellini influence

Catch-22 company on location, Guaymas, Mexico.
"For my lead shot," Willoughby recalls, "I contacted every single actor,
contacted Wardrobe, so that uniforms would be ready, contacted
Props, the Special Effects people, the labor force, and head gaffer Earl Gilbert.
Under the hot Mexican sun, reflectors would never work, so it meant
setting up arcs, which meant getting electricians laid on to run cable.
It meant arranging make-up for those not working the Saturday I planned
to shoot, and for transport to the set from Guaymas.

On Saturday the crew broke for lunch unexpectedly, and when I finally got everyone rounded up, the sun was in a different place than I'd planned, and then the smoke machine went out. And while Special Effects leaped into a Jeep to drive back for flares, Nichols was saying things like, 'What's happening, Willoughby?' and 'You know, Willoughby, if I don't like my picture you've blown the whole thing.' Now I'm trying to get everyone to concentrate on me. (I don't think Alan Arkin ever once looked at the camera.) Even at this late day, my stomach does flips when I think about that mad Saturday. But I got a good picture.''

Terror and Exhaustion: Two moods of Bree Daniels (Jane Fonda).

Klute

1971

The Cowboys

1971

Preceding pages: The cowboys were a bunch of kids
Wil Andersen (John Wayne) pressed into service for cattle drive
when he was unable to recruit an adult crew.
"Four Eyes" (Nicholas Beauvy) was one of them.
Left: Bruce Dern was "Long Hair," the bad guy.
Below: Diane Addington as one of the soiled doves of travelling
brothel run by Kate, the madam
(Colleen Dewhurst, at center on following pages).
Willoughby:
"The effort here was to recreate the feeling and appearance
of the pictures frontier photographers used to produce
with their old wet-plate cameras. It was a technical problem
that took weeks to work out, but eventually I got what
I wanted with a film that—to my knowledge—
no one has ever used for portrait photographs."

Scrofulous crew below gunned Duke down before the picture ended,
but not before he had taught his young charges how to stand up to wickedness.
Right: Another of Madam Kate's doxies (Andrea Beckett).
Following pages: Tribal portrait in frontier manner.